Todd...
my son

TERRY ODOM-MORALEZ

WITH BETTY DEEMER

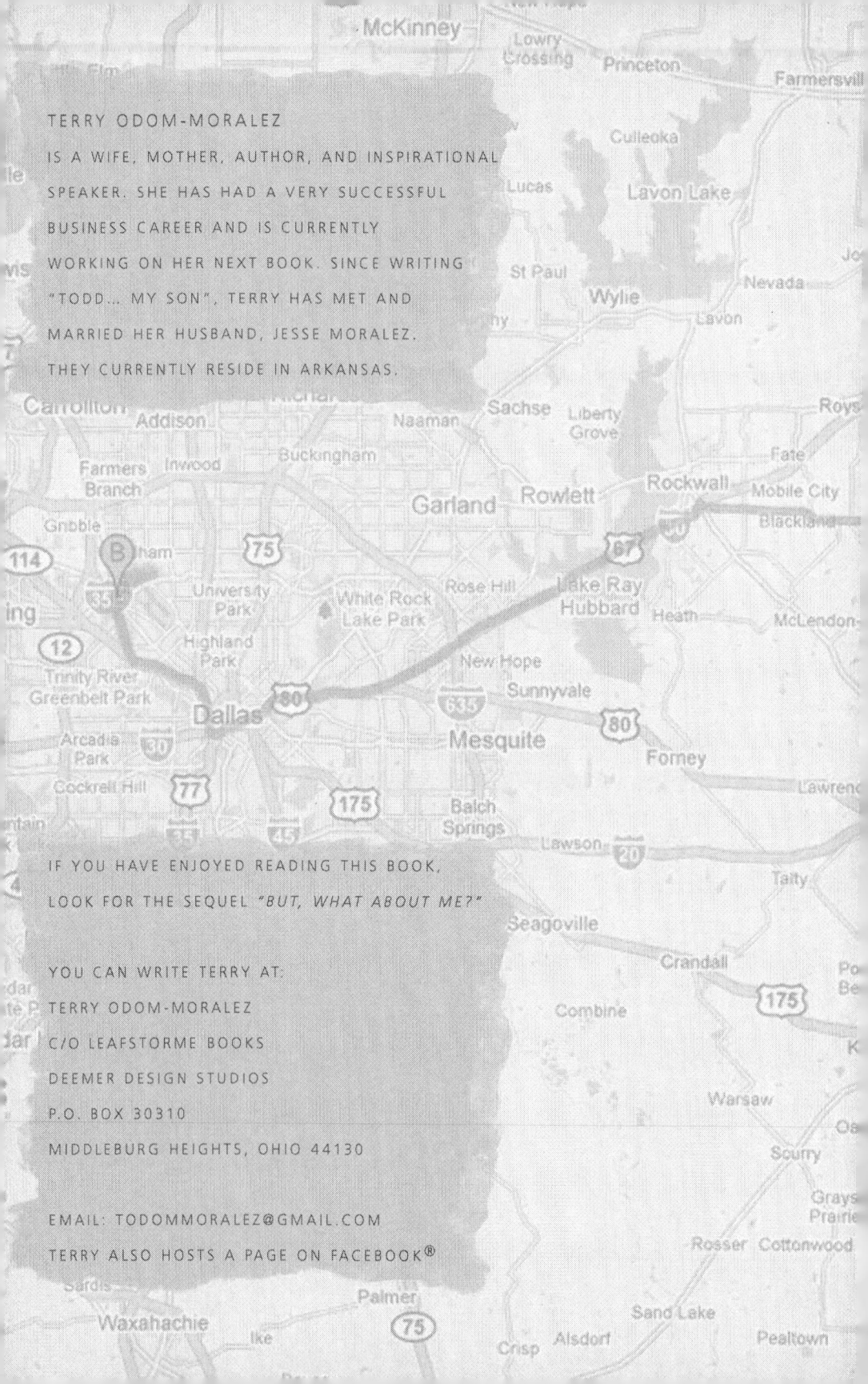

TERRY ODOM-MORALEZ
IS A WIFE, MOTHER, AUTHOR, AND INSPIRATIONAL
SPEAKER. SHE HAS HAD A VERY SUCCESSFUL
BUSINESS CAREER AND IS CURRENTLY
WORKING ON HER NEXT BOOK. SINCE WRITING
"TODD... MY SON", TERRY HAS MET AND
MARRIED HER HUSBAND, JESSE MORALEZ.
THEY CURRENTLY RESIDE IN ARKANSAS.

IF YOU HAVE ENJOYED READING THIS BOOK,
LOOK FOR THE SEQUEL *"BUT, WHAT ABOUT ME?"*

YOU CAN WRITE TERRY AT:
TERRY ODOM-MORALEZ
C/O LEAFSTORME BOOKS
DEEMER DESIGN STUDIOS
P.O. BOX 30310
MIDDLEBURG HEIGHTS, OHIO 44130

EMAIL: TODOMMORALEZ@GMAIL.COM
TERRY ALSO HOSTS A PAGE ON FACEBOOK®

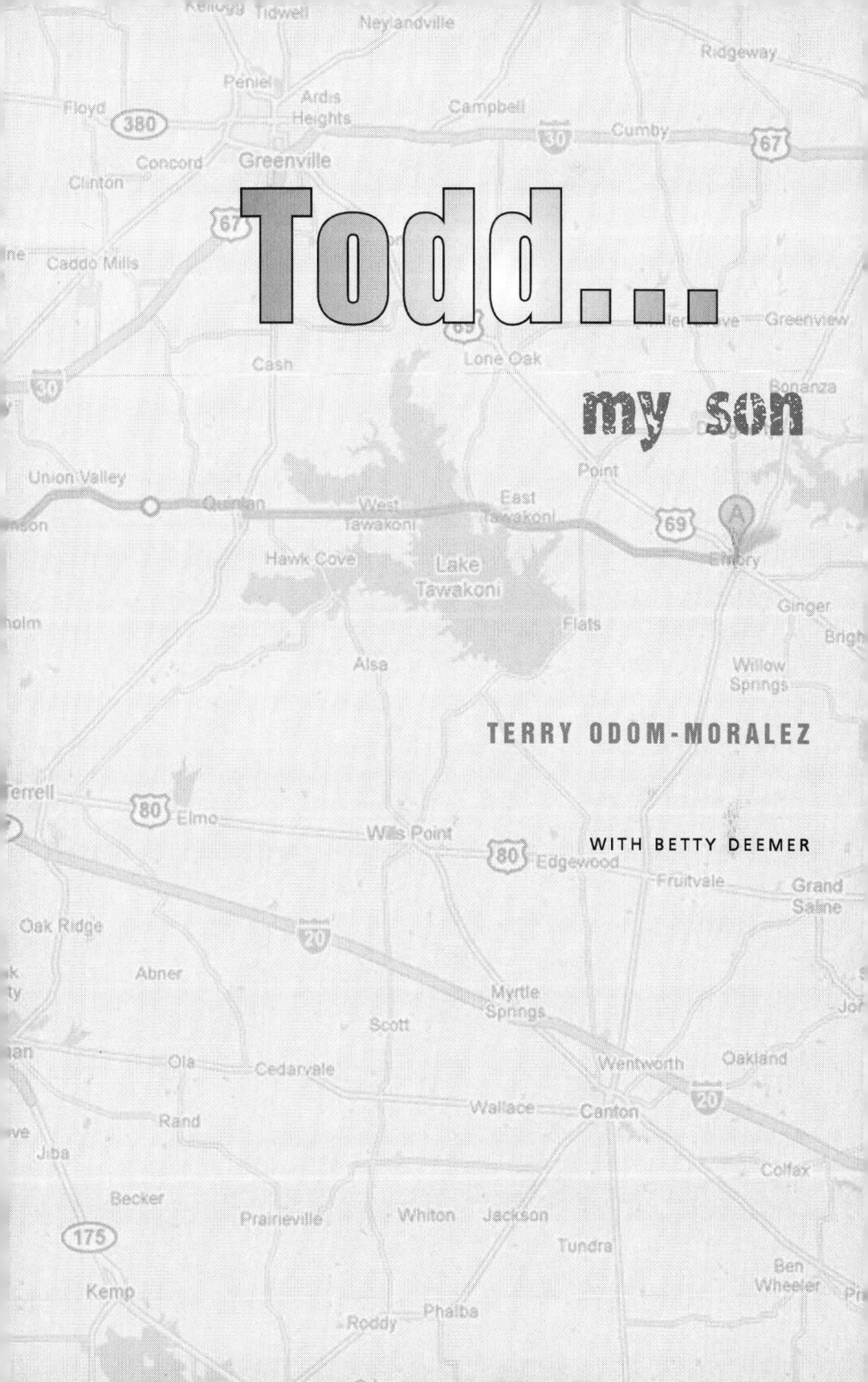

LeafStorme Books is a division of
Deemer Design Studios
P.O. Box 30310
Middleburg Heights, OH 44130

Copyright © 2009 Deemer Design Studios

All rights reserved, including the right to reproduce this
book or portions thereof in any form whatsoever.

First edition
10 9 8 7 6 5 4 3 2 1

Designed by Betty Deemer

Editor note: This story was previously published under the same title.
This new edition has been completely rewritten by the authors.

Manufactured in the United States of America

ISBN-13   978-0-9823945-0-2
ISBN-10   0-9823945-0-0

THIS BOOK IS DEDICATED TO STACY, MY DAUGHTER, WHO WAS MY ROCK DURING THE HARD TIMES, BEFORE I REALLY LEARNED TO LEAN TOTALLY UPON THE LORD — FOR ALL THE YEARS YOU LOST BECAUSE OF MY COMMITMENT TO TODD — FOR MY HAVING TO LEAVE YOU SOMETIMES TO THE MERCY OF THE WORLD — AND TO SEE YOU TODAY STANDING STRONG IN THE LORD ...

I LOVE YOU!

Mom

THANK YOU LORD FOR GIVING ME THE
VISION TO WRITE OUR STORY AND FOR NOT
LETTING THE VISION DIE — AND I THANK MY
FRIENDS FOR HELPING TO MAKE IT HAPPEN.

EDITH MEREDITH, MY STEPMOM, FOR
ENCOURAGING AND STAYING WITH ME FROM THE
BEGINNING TO THE END, AND THE LONG HOURS
OF TYPING YOU DID TO GET THE BOOK ON PAPER.

VIRGINIA LEWIS WHO EDITED THE FIRST EDITION.

LAVERNE MORRIS, YOU TAUGHT ME HOW TO
TELL A STORY WITH FEELING AND HELPED WITH
TODD IN A WAY NO ONE ELSE EVER COULD.

BETTY DEEMER WHO GAVE HER LOVE AND
CARING TOUCH TO THE PAGES OF TODD...
MY SON! HER TIME, HER ENERGY, AND
HANGING WITH ME THROUGH THE TOUGH
TIMES AND THE GOOD TIMES OF PRODUCING
AND EDITING THIS BOOK. ALL MY LOVE.

THANK YOU MOST OF ALL TO ALL THE
PEOPLE WHO SUPPORTED ME IN MY
DECISION TO FOLLOW "HIM".

LOVE TO ALL!

Terry Odom-Moralez

AND, TO JESSE. WE HAVE LOVED.
WE HAVE LASTED.

PSALM 31: 1-3 SAYS...

I HAVE TAKEN REFUGE IN HIM; THAT I SHOULD
NEVER BE ASHAMED; AND IN HIS RIGHTEOUSNESS
HE'LL DELIVER ME. HE SAID FOR ME TO INCLINE
MINE EAR AND HE'D RESCUE ME QUICKLY; HE
IS MY ROCK OF STRENGTH, A STRONG HOLD
TO SAVE ME. HE IS TRULY MY ROCK AND
MY FORTRESS.

— PARAPHRASED,
NEW INTERNATIONAL VERSION

TABLE OF CONTENTS

CHAPTER 1	THE GOOD LIFE	1
CHAPTER 2	AN UNFIRM FOUNDATION	3
CHAPTER 3	DAY TWO — OF THE REST OF OUR LIVES	7
CHAPTER 4	DAY THREE — FINDING FAITH	11
CHAPTER 5	3 WEEKS — FACING FACTS	15
CHAPTER 6	2 MONTHS — DALLAS REHABILITATION INSTITUTE	25
CHAPTER 7	4 MONTHS — SMALL HOPE AMID A LARGER PAIN	39
CHAPTER 8	5 MONTHS — WELCOME HOME	45
CHAPTER 9	WHEN REALITY SETS IN	51
CHAPTER 10	TORN ASUNDER	59
CHAPTER 11	6 - 7 MONTHS — STARTING OVER	69
CHAPTER 12	8 MONTHS — TWO INVALIDS	83
CHAPTER 13	9 MONTHS — HOME	87
CHAPTER 14	WHEN DREAMS DIE	93
CHAPTER 15	15 MONTHS — MOVIN' ON	99
CHAPTER 16	2 YEARS — CAREERS	105
CHAPTER 17	TODD'S FUTURE	107
CHAPTER 18	RISE AND WALK — MAYBE	111
CHAPTER 19	4 YEARS — SENIOR YEAR	115
CHAPTER 20	ERIC	119
CHAPTER 21	PROM	125
CHAPTER 22	GRADUATION	129
CHAPTER 23	STACY	131
CHAPTER 24	GETTING OUR FAITH BACK ON TRACK	137
CHAPTER 25	CODE RED	147
CHAPTER 26	SAYING GOODBYE	159
REMEMBERING		169
	MY FRIEND, TODD	171
PHOTO ESSAY	TODD... MY SON	173
AFTERWARD	BUT, WHAT ABOUT ME?	213

IT IS 1985. SPRING IN TEXAS IS IN FULL BLOOM. MY LIFE WITH MY HUSBAND, CLYDE, SON TODD, AND DAUGHTER STACY IS GOING WELL. EVERYONE IS HEALTHY, WE'RE ALL PRETTY HAPPY, AND LIFE SEEMS GOOD TO ME. AND THEN IT CHANGED.

YEP. THAT'S ME IN THE MIDDLE BETWEEN MY TWO SISTERS SHARON AND PEGGY.
DON'T I *LOOK* LIKE I FEEL THAT MY LIFE IS PERFECT?

CHAPTER 1
THE GOOD LIFE

I stretched and yawned as I drew a blue plaid sheet under my chin and watched Clyde* pull faded Levis over lean, sexy legs. The giggle that escaped my lips broke the silence of the house that was usually filled with the good-natured rivalry between our two teenagers. Stacy (thirteen) was visiting a friend, and Todd (fifteen) was on a camping trip with another family. It was Sunday, May 26, 1985 — Memorial Day weekend — and the kids were glad school was out. This would begin a whole summer of fun with their friends. We also planned to do some things as a family. (My parents had divorced when I was in fifth grade and I missed the closeness of family.) I not only expected this summer to be fun for my kids, but for me, too.

Having a weekend to ourselves was a rare treat. With twenty-three years of marriage ups and downs, I was feeling closer to Clyde than I had in a long time. My children and this handsome Texan were my life. The signs through those years that he was less-than-faithful faded as we enjoyed this weekend honeymoon.

Giving my foot a playful tug, Clyde left me to snuggle back under the covers while he headed for the kitchen to start the coffee.

"Hey, sleepyhead!" Clyde set my coffee cup on the table beside me. "While our time's our own, how 'bout we take a run up to the lake and see how things are going?"

"Good idea." I scooted up until I was resting against the headboard, and reached for my coffee. "We can have breakfast somewhere later."

We lived in a big sprawling house in the country near Emory, Texas, and the foundation was being poured for a liquor store we were building five miles farther up near Lake Tawakoni. The day before, giving into Clyde's wishes, I had finalized the sale of one of Merle Norman Cosmetic stores.

*In previous editions, Clyde's name was listed as "Richard."

1

The first store I had opened was in Terrell and was the larger of the two. The second smaller store was in Quinlan and I had just opened it. Clyde had been after me for some time to sell both the stores because he wanted me home with our family, but I was very uncomfortable with selling both stores at the same time. Finally, I agreed to sell the store in Terrell, but kept a ten percent ownership should I ever want to take it back.

Life had been good to us — we were financially secure and we led a good life.

That Sunday was absolutely gorgeous. A shower on Saturday had washed everything to a sparkling shine. The world looked brand new and I felt brand new. Clyde and I talked and laughed together on the short drive down to Lake Tawakoni. As I watched the beautiful profile of my husband, I felt for the first time in a very long time that... *Hey, we're going to make it. We're really going to make it.* There was not a cloud anywhere over Texas or over my family.

Reluctantly we headed toward home. The kids could be back any time, and I needed to be there when they got home. There was no way I was prepared for what lay only a few short hours away.

I was wriggling out of my too-tight jeans when the doorbell rang. Clyde opened the bedroom door just as I pulled on some comfortable jogging pants.

"Some girl is at the door, Terry," he said and gave me a puzzled look. "I don't know who she is."

Sneaker laces dangling, I followed Clyde to the door.

TODD, 14, WITH HIS TWO FAVORITE DOGS

CHAPTER 2
AN UNFIRM FOUNDATION

Tammy Watson was standing uncertainly in the doorway. (Todd was camping with Tammy's family.)

"Tammy, how are you? Come in." I cheerfully invited her into our living room.

"I'm so glad you stopped by, Tammy," I babbled. "It's been so long since I've seen you." Tammy seemed very uncomfortable, and a jolt of apprehension sliced across my midsection.

"Tammy, is anything wrong?"

"Yes," Tammy cleared her throat nervously. "There's been an accident. Todd's been hurt."

My heart dropped inside my chest. Expecting the worst, I asked her what happened.

"He was diving and he hurt his head," she explained. "But I don't think it's bad," she added hastily.

Todd had been taken to the hospital in Kaufman. I don't remember much about the hour-and-a-half trip, except that Clyde chain-smoked and drove very fast. Both of us felt Todd was seriously hurt.

The ambulance had just arrived when we got to the hospital. Clyde flipped a half-smoked cigarette onto the pavement and we rushed into the hospital corridor with its scrubbed clean smell. Clyde followed the stretcher into the emergency room. Everyone seemed to be talking at once, then suddenly I was jerked to attention, and froze, hearing the word "paralyzed".

"No! No! No! He can't be paralyzed," I moaned. My shaky legs began to buckle.

A nurse laid a comforting hand on my arm and gently washed my face with a cold cloth.

"I'm sure he's going to be all right," she said. "But for now he can't move."

When I calmed down a little, I was led into an office where I numbly filled out the necessary papers. This could not be happening. Todd was only fifteen and had just made his school's varsity football team. He was a six-foot-three-inch Rains Wildcat. He had his whole life ahead of him.

The emergency team did all they could do and decided to send him on to Baylor Hospital in Dallas. I leaned over Todd and kissed him as they wheeled his stretcher out to the waiting ambulance. People were talking around me but nothing made sense. Feeling as though I was in a vacuum, I wanted to reach out and push time backward. We needed another chance.

"Oh, Jesus," I sobbed. "I'd do better next time."

I sat beside the driver in the ambulance. I knew Clyde was just as worried as he drove our car close behind during another hour-and-a-half drive.

The screaming ambulance threaded its way through the heavy morning traffic and the wind whipping past seemed to cry in my ear — *paralyzed! Paralyzed! What would this mean for Todd? Would he walk again? Would he play football again? Would he die?*

My insides were coming apart. I tried to make conversation with the driver, wanting him to know I was in control and everything was going to be all right. My nerveless hand still clutched the washcloth the nurse had used to wash my face. I straightened my shoulders and took a deep breath. The antiseptic smell made me nauseous. I heard myself rambling on as the driver stared straight ahead. Finally, I lapsed into silence.

My mind went back to two weeks before when Todd had knee surgery so he'd be able to play football in the fall. In the waiting room, I had flipped through a magazine and an article caught my eye. A mother had written about her son who had a diving accident and became paralyzed. *Dear Jesus,* I had thought. *I could never face something like that.* The woman stated that statistically, it only happens to one in one hundred thousand. I had relaxed. That one couldn't possibly be one of my family.

My mind was jerked back to the present as the ambulance pulled up in the emergency area at Baylor. Grim faces looked down at my son, their expressions saying... *"He can't make it."*

I wanted to bury my face against Clyde, but we had to be strong and control ourselves. We waited for the doctor for what seemed like hours. When he finally examined Todd, we were not prepared for the diagnosis.

"Todd has a fracture at the cervical C-4 level."

We had no idea what that meant. But his next words were perfectly clear. His voice was firm and practiced.

"Todd is paralyzed from his neck down." Then came the final hammer blow. "Your son will never regain any movement."

I felt as if my breath had been sucked right out of my chest. I glanced at Todd, seeing his beautiful green eyes filled with rage. Before the doctor came, Todd had been angry because he was strapped down, the ambulance team had made him immobile.

"Get me up from here, my head is killing me," he had begged us. Now he lay there while this doctor stripped him of any hope.

The doctor looked straight at Todd.

"Todd, you will never walk again."

Clyde held his tongue until the doctor left the room, but his clenched fist and red face revealed his anger.

"Todd, you don't have to listen to what that doctor says. We know you will walk again."

Clyde and Todd felt his injury was only temporary. They believed Todd would be in the Wildcat lineup in the fall. I wanted to join them in their belief that Todd would recover, but I knew... I knew what being paralyzed would mean.

Like a zombie, I walked through the hours while Todd was being re-examined and decisions were being made. First, there would be surgery on his neck. Then they found surgery might not be needed, only traction — Todd's neck was dislocated not broken. I flinched as tongs were surgically placed in Todd's skull and 40 lbs. of weights were arranged for traction. It looked horrible, but Todd began to settle down as pressure was relieved. Because of the paralysis, he had not been given anything for pain or the trauma he was going through. Though only fifteen, Todd was taking it like a man.

Those first hours passed in a blur of white coats and machines. We had called our families, and that first night outside the Intensive Care Unit, my dad and stepmother, my sister Sharon and her minister, and Clyde's sister and her husband were with us to pray and watch the door to the room where my son lay confused and very, very helpless because he could not move anything from the neck down.

However — even though he was flat on his back — the one thing Todd could still do was eat. He had not lost his ability to swallow or his growing-boy appetite. Even as, he lay stiff and straight with his head stretched back in traction, those horrible tongs sticking out of his head, and weighted down with forty pounds of weight — he could still eat and he was still very hungry. In the midst of all that emergency, Todd consumed a lot of hamburgers and fries. Funny, the things we remember.

TODD, 15 — AT OVER 6'3" HE WAS STILL A GROWING BOY
(CLYDE, STACY, TODD)

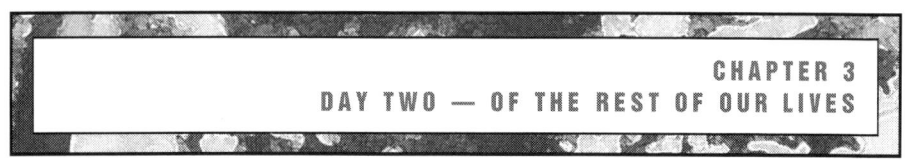

CHAPTER 3
DAY TWO — OF THE REST OF OUR LIVES

Word of Todd's accident had reached his friends and schoolmates, and many of them drove to Baylor. They huddled quietly, waiting with sober young faces. That this could happen to someone their age stunned them to silence.

We were all trying to cope with our emotions in one way or another. Clyde paced and lit each new cigarette off his last one. Unbidden tears were quickly wiped away as we tried to encourage each other, especially Todd.

"We know you're going to be all right. You just hang tight."

Muffled night sounds gradually gave way to the quiet of early morning chatter as shifts changed and the hospital settled in for another routine day — and we tried to ready ourselves for whatever lay ahead.

As the jumble of that first day turned into the second we wearily realized we needed rest. The nurses assured us they would call if Todd needed us. Stacy, Clyde and I were soon taking much needed showers in the hotel adjoining the hospital. But sleep eluded us. We lay wide awake.

"He's going to be all right," Clyde said as he swung his long legs over the side of the king size bed and lit another cigarette.

As I sat up and gently began rubbing his back, I mumbled agreement, but was really unconvinced. Stroking my husband's tense shoulders I wondered silently... *Will he really? What must he be thinking right now? About the things that's been taken away from him? His football career? What must he be feeling? Is he thinking he will never play ball again?*

When Todd was born, he weighed almost 10 pounds — a bigger-than-average baby — and as he grew, he was much bigger than other boys his age. There was always the problem of finding clothes big enough for his tall, husky body. Pictures of Todd running and laughing played across my mind.

A sob threatened to escape my tight throat. But I had to be strong. I couldn't give way to the hysteria that lay quivering in the pit of my stomach. We all were trying to deal with the magnitude of what we were facing, and we had to remember that what Todd was facing was so much more than we could imagine. He was the one who would never be able to eat by himself again, or tie his shoes, or brush his teeth. He would always depend on someone else for his every need. Unless… unless Clyde was right. Maybe he would be all right. A twinge of hope tried to rise up in my heart, but the faith I needed would not rise to meet it. Somehow, deep inside, I knew Todd would never be all right, but I knew I could never voice that belief to Clyde.

"Honey," I said, resting my chin on his shoulder. "Remember how proud Todd was when he suited up that first time?"

"Yep," Clyde choked, taking a long drag on his umpteenth cigarette.

Finally, we fell asleep from sheer exhaustion, but before long we were back downstairs checking on Todd. We found him very angry. He had called the nurse, but she hadn't kept her promise to call us.

Sometime in the stillness of the night after we had gone to the hotel, Todd had come face to face with reality. Helpless frustration had given way to panic and he thought he was losing his mind.

"Mom, pray for me. Please pray for me."

I realized at that moment how far I had wandered from any relationship with God. My life had become so wrapped up in my family, I didn't need anyone else — I could cope with whatever problem came along. And now my precious son needed something I couldn't give him. I wasn't even sure if God would hear my prayer. Quietly I bowed my head and said a simple prayer.

"Please, God. Help Todd. He needs you. Thank you."

We were both sobbing.

"Mom, I'm so scared. What's gonna happen to me?"

Although Todd could move nothing, I felt his need to cling to me as he did when he was a child and woke up from a bad dream. But this was no childish fear and it was no bad dream. He would not wake up from this. We were all facing something that would be there tomorrow and next week and next year. I could feel panic rising inside me.

I can't handle this, I thought. *I love Todd with all my being but this is too hard. He can't move at all. He can't even raise his arm to scratch his own nose.*

There was absolutely no movement. I was thankful that he could talk and eat, but that did little to assuage the strange things I was beginning to feel. I wanted to run. I couldn't eat. I couldn't drink. I couldn't even think. Seeing Todd became harder and harder for me. Only two days and I wanted to give up.

Friends kept trying to encourage us.

"Gee, Todd looks good."

"Hey, he'll be back at school before you know it."

I didn't want to hear it.

Later that day, a friend from home came with her husband who was confined to a wheelchair.

"I know what you're going through," she said. "I know about paralysis and what it means to have a permanent injury." She went on to tell us about handicap tags and the bladder situation.

I knew she was trying to be helpful but the minute she turned her head, I walked out without looking back. I paced the halls and cried. After a couple of hours I had enough control to call Clyde to see if she was gone.

"Yes, she's gone," he said. "Terry, you were so rude."

"I couldn't help it. I can't deal with now, and I sure can't handle the future."

"You didn't have to listen," said Clyde. "That's not going to happen to Todd."

Clyde refused to entertain even the remote possibility that our son would not walk away from this horror. He couldn't deal with his heartache. Anything less than complete recovery for Todd was something he would not accept.

"Terry, you've got to get control of yourself," Clyde whispered. "He needs us now, and he needs to know everything's going to be all right."

But, that's just the point, I thought as I wearily ran my hands through my short hair. *Todd's life is over. It just got started and it's over.*

I was weak from lack of food but the thought of eating was repulsive. I felt completely out of control and had the sensation of being totally inward — like I was being tucked away inside myself.

Somehow, we made it through that second day, then trudged in silence back to our room to try to sleep. We had nothing to say to each other — we were too numb.

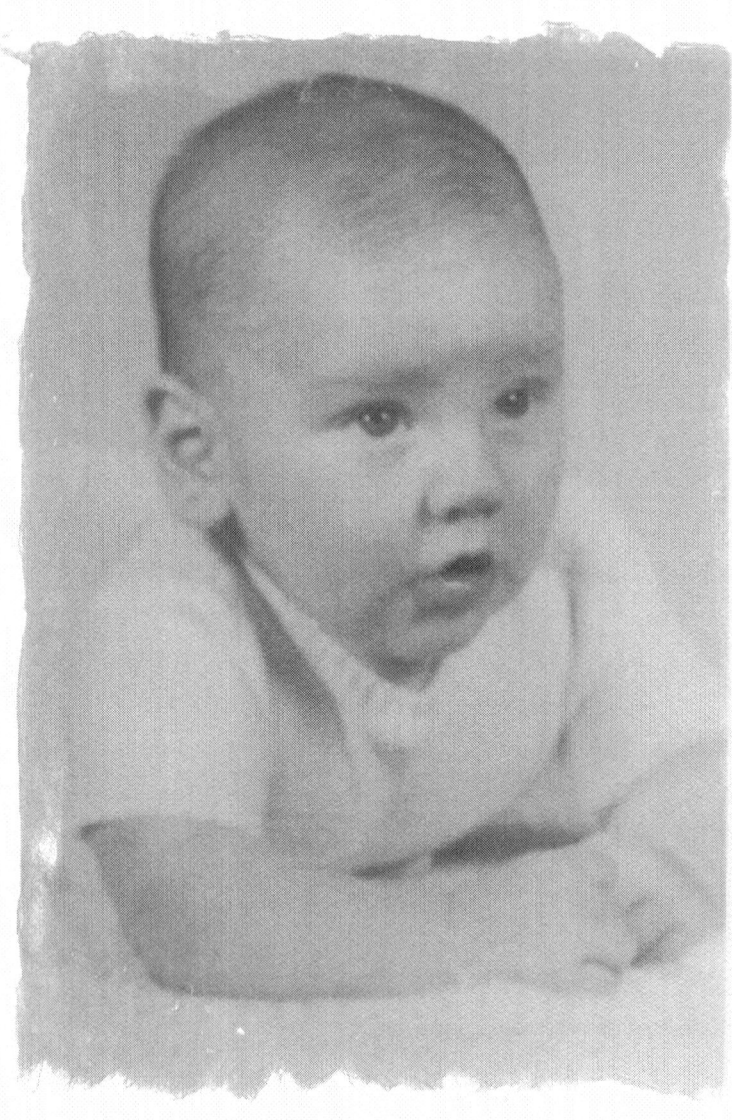

TODD WEIGHED OVER 10 LBS.
WHEN HE WAS BORN AND QUICKLY GREW!

CHAPTER 4
DAY THREE — FINDING FAITH

I woke around two a.m. All I could think was that Todd would never play ball again. We'd never see him in a lineup with his team mates. This was such a loss, not only for Todd, but for me. I hadn't realized before how proud I was of him, or how much a part of me he was. I had watched as he worked to control his big strong body so he might someday be a professional player. As I lay there, it never crossed my mind that he could die, only that he would never be the same again — he'd never play ball again!

I quietly dressed without waking Clyde or Stacy. I had to get out of the room — I needed to be alone.

Tears streaming down my face, I stumbled into the hall and onto the elevator. Somehow, I ended up in the basement of the hospital, totally disoriented. I felt as though I was bouncing from one wall to the other. A security guard found me leaning against the cold bare wall, weeping.

"Ma'am, can I help you?" His concern only brought more tears. "Ma'am, is there anything I can do?" He repeated

"Could you take me to a chaplain?" I finally sobbed out.

"I sure can," he said. "Follow me."

The guard led me to a room nearby and helped me to a chair. He said he'd be back in a minute, and I heard him lock the door behind him. I sat crying for what seemed an eternity. I was still crying when the chaplain came in and sat beside me.

"Can I help you?" he asked.

"I don't know if anyone can help me," I said. "But I'd sure like to just talk to you."

I then began to pour out my heart. Everything that had happened the last two days came spilling out with a voice muffled by tears. All the pain and confusion Todd was suffering, and the fear and hurt we were all going through.

"I don't know if I even believe in God anymore!" I spat the words out unexpectedly. "I have reached the point in my life where I've just chosen to be what my husband wants — and I'm just not sure anymore if God even exists!"

Angrily, I told this stranger about the year before when Clyde was involved with another woman. I had loved Clyde so much, yet I knew I could no longer put myself or my kids through the torment of living with a man who was constantly having affairs. Our lives were on a continuous up and down cycle. I put Clyde under a peace bond so he couldn't get to me, and filed for divorce.

At first I was relieved because I no longer had to worry about where Clyde was or what he was doing — but the kids and I were left alone on Lake Tawakoni to begin life alone and I was now single.

I became lonely, and began going out with friends to have a good time and to drown my sorrows. Todd (fourteen) and Stacy (twelve) were too young to understand how lonely I really was. Something was missing from my life, but I didn't know what. The more I ran, the more miserable I became, and the less control I had over the kids.

My mind was racing as I poured out my heart to the chaplain.

I remembered one spring afternoon when Todd and Stacy had begged to go swimming. I'd been miserable that day. They just wanted to have some fun, yet I knew the lake was much too cold for swimming, and that partic-

THE BRIDGE OVER LAKE TAWAKONI

ular day, it was too rough. Finally, I gave in and let them go. Later, I walked down to the water's edge to check on them.

The water seemed eerie with a haze that made it hard to see. My eyes searched the dark water that was splashing hard against the bank. I saw yellow and blue towels strewn carelessly near the water, but couldn't see Todd or Stacy. Throwing away my soda, I ran to see if they had wandered over to play with the neighbor's twins. They weren't there.

Seldom given to hysterics — this time I panicked. Running quickly back to the house, I dialed my mother's number.

"The kids have drowned! The kids have drowned!" I screamed into the phone.

"Terry, calm down. Calm down and call the fire department," my mother said. (My step-dad had been a fireman, so naturally my mother knew just what I needed to do.)

I fumbled with the telephone and finally connected with the fire department. Trying to be calm, I began to give them directions to our lake home. Then through the window, I saw in the far distance, two little heads bobbing in the water.

"Wait just a minute. Wait just a minute! I think I can see them just coming around the bend. Yes! Yes! I can see them!" Relief washed over me and I ran out of the house down to the water's edge.

"Where have you been? I couldn't see you. I thought you had drowned," I cried, reaching for the two shivering bodies.

"We've been right here," they said in unison.

At that moment, I felt that there was a power much higher than mine trying to get my attention. I knew something had changed in my life. That night, unable to sleep, I found myself praying for God to give me direction. I knew my children needed both a mama and a daddy. Before that week was over, Clyde and I began working out our problems and decided to stop the divorce.

I had sworn I would never stray from the Lord again. I wanted to stay close to Him, but before long, I found myself once again becoming so involved with my husband and children that nothing else mattered.

The chaplain's voice penetrated the fog in which my mind was wandering — just as God had tried to penetrate my life back there at Lake Tawakoni when I thought I had lost my children. Now, even as I denied the existence of God with my mouth, my heart knew the truth. There really was a God. There was *someone* to help me through what we were going through.

I had been with the Chaplain for several hours and left the room feeling as if I had been reborn. I went back upstairs, refreshed and with a new attitude. But the brand new hope that had sprung up in my being was soon put to the test.

"We haven't gotten the alignment we need, so we'll have to operate," the doctor told us. Then he added grimly, "There's a good possibility Todd won't live through it."

I'm sure my smile must have puzzled the doctor, but something wonderful was happening. I knew everything would be all right. My faith was high. This would be Todd's first major surgery and he would have to have it because the "alignment" the doctors were hoping would happen by surgically implanting tongs into his head and adding weights, had not worked. (He would eventually have this surgery, but not at Baylor.)

That evening in our hotel room, Stacy, Clyde and I knelt together. I prayed, asking the Lord to come into our lives and to help us get through this. I knew we couldn't do it without Him. I didn't ask for Todd to walk, but for God to guide us through whatever lay ahead.

Back at the hospital — the forty pounds of pressure had brought the realignment necessary in his neck, so no surgery would be needed at that point. The timing had been a miracle. Was it because of answered prayer?

Now that we were through that crisis, the doctors began talking about sending him to their Rehab Center. We were ready for the next step.

CHAPTER 5
3 WEEKS — FACING FACTS

It had been almost three weeks since Todd's accident.

Personnel from the hospital took Clyde and me across the street to Baylor's Rehab Center so we could see what it would be like. We entered a dreary gray-walled room filled with people in wheelchairs. Some were worse than others, but they had one thing in common, they each wore a beautiful smile. I felt if we could get Todd to this point, he could make it. I was very optimistic, but Clyde still struggled with his emotions. He had finally come face to face with the fact that Todd would likely never walk again.

It seemed as if Clyde had been leaning more on my faith than his own. He had no relationship with God, and now, as my faith was getting stronger, Clyde was at the end of his strength and had nothing else to tap into.

A new thought came to me and (feeling a little stupid), I questioned a therapist.

"Will Todd be able to father a child?"

"Probably, a little further down the line," he answered.

I knew we'd have to deal with that later, but at least it was a possibility. Right now though, we had to get him as far as he could go with what he had.

But, Todd seemed to be getting more and more angry. He acted strangely, unlike himself. He talked like he was out of his head.

"He's having trouble breathing," the doctor explained.

Todd was given more oxygen, but the doctor felt his anger and strange behavior were because he had been in ICU for such a long time — most of the three weeks since his accident.

Soon, there was talk about moving Todd out of ICU and into a private room in the pulmonary section of the hospital. I was elated. If we could get a room where we could be together, we'd be okay — so, I kept asking the head nurse of that department if we could move to a suite, rather than just a plain room. I guess I was becoming something of a nuisance to her, but I just knew that I had to keep my family together to help us and to help Todd as well.

I took it upon myself to begin to shop around in the hospital for just the right room that would accommodate my family — not knowing that what I was doing would be perceived by same head nurse as trying to circumvent her authority. A girl I knew worked in the admitting office and I explained our situation to her. Eager to help, she showed me a beautiful and peaceful suite that would be perfect for all of us.

However, the head nurse was very put out with me by what she saw as me "going over her head" and she coldly led us to a room on the pediatric floor. Of course, at fifteen, Todd still fit into that category, but he was far from being a child, measuring over six-feet-tall and still weighing in at over two hundred and sixty pounds!

The room they gave us was old and dilapidated. There was a sad looking couch that didn't even make into a bed — two of us would have to

1983-84 8TH GRADE WILDCATS:
ROBBIE LEWELLING, TIM NORTHCUTT, SHANNON SHEPPARD, LANCE EILAND, TODD ODOM (NO. 75), JOE BLACK, JEFF WATSON, MICHAEL WILSON, BRIAN RECER, KENT KILE, HALBERT ROBINSON, DERRICK MCMILLAN, LANCE LUSK, HEATH SISK, BRANAON JONES, LEE BLANTON, SCOTT LAND, CLIFFORD MCMILLIAN, STEVE MCNEIL, SHANE WORLEY, LANCE HOOTEN TIMMY JENNINGS, SIDNEY BARKER KYLE COKER, MIKEY WILSON, LARRY CORK, BILLY LUCKETT

sleep on the floor. We were furious. But at least it was private, and we would be together.

Different types of beds were tried out on Todd. The doctors decided on a rotating bed (in spinal cord injuries, the patient has to keep turning). Rather than having a nurse turn him every few hours, Todd was put in a bed that would rotate. They didn't even put clothes on him, just covered his private area with a towel and put a sheet over him. The bed would rotate from side-to-side in a constant motion.

Spinal cord injuries were fairly new in treatment. (We later learned Baylor Hospital was not equipped as well as it should have been for such treatment; to some extent, they were really experimenting.)

Todd couldn't sleep except for when they came in to give him his breathing treatment. For five days and nights, Clyde and I stood vigil over him. The rotating bed moved from side-to-side. Hour after hour, we took turns placing a wet washcloth on his head to keep him cool from the high fever.

I was tired... Clyde was tired... And we were getting no help from the staff because they felt we were interfering. It was a constant battle.

The staff at Baylor kept insisting that there was nothing wrong with Todd except "ICU Syndrome," a form of delirium or brain fever. They thought we were just trying to spoil him but in reality, we knew our son, and we knew that something was going terribly wrong with him. The more we balked and asked for help, the more the staff at Baylor refused to give him good treatment.

Todd kept getting more and more irate with each passing day. He no longer even reacted like himself. That wonderful son of ours had turned into a raving maniac, hallucinating and talking out of his head. Time and time again, we told the doctors about his reactions — to no avail.

"This is not uncommon," they explained. "As we told you earlier, Todd is suffering from what is called ICU Syndrome. It should pass in a few days."

Clyde and I watched Todd getting worse and worse. We knew this was not normal. We sat by his bed night and day holding his head and listening to him talking crazy.

"Mama, I want to go home!" he would yell. In his delirium, he saw steaks falling from the ceiling, and he'd tell us he was taking us out to eat.

In my desperation, I remembered the article I had read about Alana Shepherd's son who had also been paralyzed in a diving accident. She had established a spinal cord research center in Atlanta, Georgia. I reminded Clyde of the article.

"Clyde, we need to call that center and see if we can move Todd to Atlanta. Maybe they could turn this around. At least it's better than just letting him die!"

Clyde was ready to do whatever it took.

Doctors at the Shepherd Center in Atlanta, Georgia felt Todd could be airlifted to Atlanta without risk. Clyde and I made plans to go there to make arrangements for the transfer.

We were up with Todd the whole night before we left. He was extremely bad, but the staff refused to help us with him. I felt they were just

AS I FELT THE PLANE LEAVING THE GROUND AND HEADING FOR GEORGIA — I REALIZED THAT FOR THE FIRST TIME IN MY LIFE, I WAS NOT AFRAID TO FLY.

letting him die. Clyde and I felt they were punishing him because of us and hired a private nurse to stay with Todd the ten hours we would be gone. Our daughter Stacy, Clyde's mother, and his sister were also staying.

That next morning, Clyde and I barely made the plane — the doors shut behind us as we climbed aboard.

As I felt the plane leaving the ground heading for Georgia, I realized that for the first time in my life, I was not afraid to fly. In fact, I would have loved for that plane to crash. I wanted out of this misery. But God had other plans. My stepmother Edie and I had prayed before we left — asking the Lord to let us know by a warm assurance if this move was right for Todd.

All the way from the airport in a cab, I felt the Spirit of God, but once I was inside Shepherd's, even though it was beautiful, to me it just felt cold. I felt this was not the place for Todd, but Clyde was still very excited about the center.

"This is where Todd needs to be, Terry. He'll get better here." It seemed Clyde and I were never quite in sync.

We filled out the necessary papers, then took a cab back to the airport for our return to Baylor Hospital in Dallas. We had been gone from Baylor twelve hours.

As we stepped off the elevator on the pediatric floor, to our surprise, the whole family was in the waiting room. My heart stopped and I groped for Clyde's hand.

"He's gone!" I felt my heart tremble. But they were all smiling.

"What's happened?" I asked.

With everyone talking at once, we learned Todd had actually died while we were gone and had to be resuscitated. The staff had brought in the emergency equipment and brought Todd back to life. They had to put an airway through his nose and into his lungs so he could breathe.

I knew it! I knew it! He couldn't breathe. Clyde and I were right all along, I thought to myself.

"You've got to see him," Stacy said.

For the first time in five days, Todd was finally able to sleep. Smiling through my tears, I watched Todd, his face like an angel, sleeping peacefully.

I knew then for the first time, I could let him go — but Todd's story was not to end there.

We phoned Shepherd Center in Atlanta the next morning. Having been kept abreast of Todd's condition, they told us that under the circumstances, it would be impossible to move him. They told us there was another spinal cord center in Dallas and gave us the name of a Dr. Wharton at Dallas Rehabilitation Institute who would be willing to take over Todd's case.

We met with the Baylor doctors who had worked with Todd to advise them of our intentions to move Todd to St. Paul Hospital (the hospital used by Dallas Rehab for their intensive care patients until they could be moved to their Rehab Center).

The Baylor doctors were very understanding. As we talked in the quiet room provided for critical situations, they were very cooperative and eager to help. It was only later that we learned why.

Dr. Wharton came to Baylor that afternoon and looked at Todd's X-rays. He took us aside and told us Todd was in critical condition.

"Todd's got lots of problems," Dr. Wharton said grimly. "Some very serious breathing problems."

He explained that during the days when Todd was having such a hard time breathing, he kept pulling up with his head which caused his neck to come out of alignment.

"Now Todd has a second spinal cord injury," Dr. Wharton said "The level of feeling he had has gone from his chest to his chin."

I was sick, really sick. *How could the staff at Baylor have let this happen? How much more could we take?*

"After we have stabilized his lungs," Dr. Wharton continued. "We'll have to do surgery to realign his neck. And that's just the first in the process of getting him up and mobile. It's possible his level of feeling will return," Dr. Wharton offered hopefully.

He couldn't make any promises. We'd just have to wait and see. This would be Todd's second surgery — the first was to put the tongs directly into his skull and attach the weights.

Todd's transfer came early the next morning. Clyde stayed by his side while the staff made preparations for the ambulance to transport him to

St. Paul. Clyde had become obsessed with the notion he should stay with Todd all the time — as if his presence would somehow infuse strength into Todd's body. He hadn't given up the idea that Todd would walk — he wanted it so badly.

This time, Clyde would ride with Todd in the ambulance. I quickly ran back to the hotel and threw our things in a bag. As fast as I could,

TODD, LITTLE LEAGUE FOOTBALL TEAM

I rushed to the car, tossed the bag inside and took off hurrying to get behind the ambulance.

We can handle this, I thought as I felt my faith getting stronger. *It might be very hard, but I'm going to figure out a way for us all to be together, then everything will be all right.* I still felt that if all four of us could be in the same room together, we'd make it.

Baylor staff loaded Todd into the ambulance. The transfer was going faster and more smoothly than we expected. The trip to St. Paul hospital was done with red lights flashing and sirens going.

As I reached the hospital, I quickly parked the car and ran to the emergency entrance. They had already taken Todd to the ICU and I was sent to prepare the paper work to admit him. When I reached Clyde in the waiting room outside of ICU, he told me that, in the ambulance Todd had another one of the breathing spells that had almost taken his life while he and I were in Atlanta.

We were not allowed to see him until the St. Paul staff had him settled in ICU. We didn't question them — we were just so relieved to have Todd in this place where we felt he would be treated by people who knew what they were doing.

Todd seemed to feel more secure. He had a big grin on his face when we went in to see him, and he was eager for them to get his neck stabilized. We thought the surgery would be right away, but we didn't realize then how bad his lungs were. They immediately began treatment for his lungs.

That first night at St. Paul, Clyde and I took turns sitting beside Todd — something we had not been allowed to do at Baylor while he was in ICU. He was once again on a rotating bed — we were starting all over from scratch.

Todd was burning up with fever. Once again we would wet a washcloth and hold it on his forehead as the bed would rock from side-to-side. I had to stand on a chair because the bed was so high, and reach over him. Clyde and I became very tired because Todd wanted one of us in the room with him at all times.

There was no hotel at St. Paul, but a case worker told us we qualified to stay at Ronald McDonald House. (For a family to qualify, the patient had to be fifteen or younger and be seriously ill.) Ronald McDonald House was in walking distance of the hospital and was very convenient for us. We were also able to encourage others and be encouraged ourselves. It was comforting just to know we were not alone, that others were facing similar crises — some other families were having to face the problems of dealing with deformities or brain damage in their children.

"Honey," I told Clyde one day as we walked across the parking lot. "At least Todd has a strong mind, and if we can help him use that, he can live a fairly normal life."

Clyde snorted.

"Normal! He won't even be close." He sailed a half-smoked cigarette on to the pavement. "I just wish we could have some privacy."

That first weekend at St. Paul, we waited anxiously for Monday when they planned to do the surgery that would stabilize Todd's neck. A day or two after the operation, Todd would go to Dallas Rehab. The doctor said they would soon make him get up.

Get up, I thought. *He can't even sit up. Why can't you just let him rest?*

Aching for him, I felt that Todd should just be given the time to recuperate, but I had to trust that the St. Paul staff knew the right things to do. Todd's lungs were not clear enough Monday. Once again, surgery had to be postponed.

We went through the next few days in a "twilight zone." There was no rest for us as we sat beside Todd day and night. We felt batted back and forth between meetings with doctors. Tears were always close to the surface, but there was seldom any time to let go.

During this time, a couple of football players and coaches on Todd's team came to see him. Although to us it seemed an eternity since his accident, it had really had not been that long since Todd had been the strapping football player everyone remembered.

Clyde didn't want the boys to go in.

"I think it'll be good for Todd," I said. "It'll give him a lift, and he could use a lift."

I was wrong.

The boys tried to keep a stiff upper lip as they visited with Todd. Todd tried to be brave, but the visit didn't last long.

After they left, I stood by Todd's bed while tears streamed down his face. All I could do was hold him and wipe them away. It was the first time he had really allowed himself to cry. I had no words to say. I couldn't encourage him, because at that point, I didn't believe he would ever walk again. Even though my heart was breaking, I felt the Spirit of God pouring a strength into me, readying me for an unknown future. For now, all Clyde and I could do was stand beside Todd and cry with him.

Monday, June 10, 1985

Frustration...

Todd & I openly wept & cried. First time he has cried. I think he is thinking more clearly and he realizes what this condition actually may be.

Earlier went to my room – thought maybe it would help with the depression and feeling of helplessness I was feeling. Started opening bills and discovered one of the envelopes brought to me was the title to his pickup that we had gotten him for his birthday. It was in his name only, Todd Edward Odom. That was not all – in the next envelope I opened was the bill for the crutches he had used in his knee surgery two weeks before his accident.

Guess it was a mistake to try and face reality. I got on my knees and asked God to give me strength and endurance.

Then I came back to Todd's room more depressed than ever. (This is when Todd and I talked and prayed that Jesus would give us the strength to get through this horrible mess.)

EXCERPT FROM TERRY'S DIARY

CHAPTER 6
2 MONTHS — DALLAS REHABILITATION INSTITUTE

The day finally came when Todd was able to have surgery. We were all happy to know that soon his neck would be stabilized and he would soon be on his way to Dallas Rehab. Maybe we could have a place to live together as a family. Maybe Todd could be moved to Atlanta. We reached for any kind of hope.

We cried as we watched Todd being wheeled to surgery. We knew he could die.

"See you later!" Todd flashed a smile at us, but I saw the tinge of fear that lay behind those beautiful eyes.

After four long hours we were told the operation was successful. We didn't even ask about his spinal cord, not wanting to hear that it had been severed. Todd was very sick when he regained consciousness — we were right back to square one! But, with plans being made to take him to Dallas Rehab, Todd didn't have time to rest, or even to be sick.

Dallas Rehab resembled an old nursing home. It was depressing, but we knew we could stand it until we moved him to Atlanta.

Todd could not breathe on his own, so a ventilator breathed for him — and would possibly do it the rest of his life, we were told.

"No way," I told Clyde and Stacy. "He might go home paralyzed, but he won't take the ventilator."

I personally had not been looking forward to going to Dallas Rehab because we were told we could not spend nights in Todd's room.

Finally, we were at Dallas Rehab and Todd was taken from the ambulance straight to their ICU. Shocked, I looked around the tiny room. There were four beds separated by curtains. Profanities were coming from one of the beds where a teenage boy was tied down. He had been in a car accident, and now lay helpless, ranting and raving. Another bed held a teenage boy, injured in a three-wheeler accident.

The control I had managed so far finally broke and I fled to the hall where I let my tears go.

We were free to come and go as we pleased in ICU, which helped, but the place was so depressing to me. Everyone was in a wheelchair, or had a head injury. Most were unable to speak and many were helplessly drooling. I *had* to believe things would get better for Todd.

[I have to say, as you can see from what you've just read, that at first, I really, really hated Dallas Rehab and could not wait until Todd was well enough for us to send him to Atlanta. Why? Because it was so depressing to see people as they aren't meant to be seen. Young and old alike — people were in this place who could no longer help themselves.

But, I also grew to love Dallas Rehab because of the love and care that Todd received. Eventually, I no longer saw an old and decrepit building, but a refuge for myself and Todd.]

A beautiful teenager named Carlotta began to talk with us once in awhile in the waiting room. A paraplegic, Carlotta was unable to walk but could use her arms and hands. Just like every other doting mother, I bragged about Todd — how handsome and special he was. Carlotta wanted to meet him.

Todd hadn't yet reached the age to care about girls, or so I thought. Anyway, he was not his charming self with Carlotta. He seemed, and he acted, bored and irritable. We learned later that this was a natural reaction for his condition. The truth was, he couldn't breathe, and he was scared — but all in all, he was just plain embarrassed in front of Carlotta. (I found out later that he had been the "mucho macho" man with girls at school and now here was this beautiful young girl encouraging him and he just wanted to fade away.)

Putting our lives on hold, we spent as much time with Todd as possible. There were times when he was irritable with all of us. One weekend, he was especially hostile. He didn't say much, it was just his expression, so miserably unhappy. We tried to cheer him up, pushing his wheelchair wherever he wanted to go, but that day it just wasn't working.

"Just take me back to bed. Mama, make them let me go to bed," he kept grumbling.

> Saturday, June 29, 1985
>
> Not much happening. Todd is in his chair and we are able to roll him around. He spent his first night in the Iron Lung. But did not rest well.

> Sunday, June 30th
>
> Another Sunday – 5 weeks today. Todd's anxious they are trying to wean him from the ventilator so they can remove the tracheotomy from his throat. Every night he goes into the Iron Lung so they can take the breathing machine off. The Iron Lung breathes for him, however, he's still complaining that he cannot get enough air!
>
> So frustrating because as parents what do we know about oxygen? They make him get up first thing into the chair; He's been begging all day to go back to bed. He's so very tired and they won't let him because they say he needs to stay up. Clyde finally loses his cool with Todd and tells him he's going to have to try and help himself. Looks like we could have seen the writing on the wall. Finally he eats a good supper so he can go back to bed at 6 PM. Still being back in the Iron Lung he complains of not enough air. But he drifts off to sleep. All day while in his chair we hold a mouth piece in his mouth so he could sleep.

EXCERPTS FROM TERRY'S DIARY

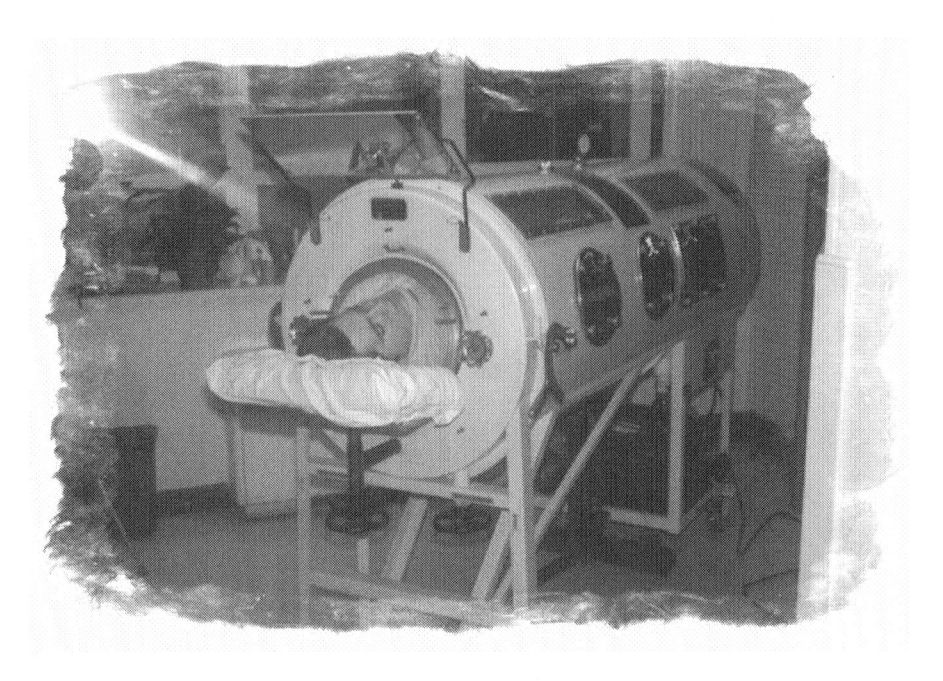

TODD IN IRON LUNG — JUST BEFORE HE WAS TAKEN OFF THE RESPIRATOR
(HE ONLY HAD TO SLEEP IN IRON LUNG AT NIGHT FOR A SHORT TIME
WHILE THEY WEANED HIM OFF THE RESPIRATOR)

We had no control over what the Dallas Rehab staff did with Todd. They knew best, and we were afraid they'd send us home if we made a fuss. Clyde lost it with Todd for the first time.

"Todd, it's time you straightened up. We're all in this together, and we're trying to make the best of it. You have to, too."

Todd did behave himself a little better and we made it through the rest of the weekend. If we could only have known that Todd was really not responsible for his behavior, but how could we have known?

Back at Ronald McDonald House, Clyde decided to go home to get some work done. It was an hour and half drive back to Emory. Emory is 75 miles through Dallas traffic and then onto the freeway — sometimes the drive could take a good two hours. However, before he could leave, we got a phone call that there was an emergency with Todd. Now that he had been moved to Dallas Rehab, we were about five minutes away from him. We jumped into the car and sped to Dallas Rehab, only to once again see an ambulance backed up to carry him back to St. Paul. The staff had papers for us to sign to release him back to the hospital. No one seemed to know what was wrong. I heard someone say as they came out of ICU, "He's blind."

No! I cried silently. *He can't be blind, too. Was it never to end?*

We learned that Todd had once again died and had to be resuscitated — just like at Baylor. They loaded him once more into the ambulance and, with sirens screaming, rushed him to St. Paul.

> Monday, July 1st
>
> Can't believe it's another month. Got a call first thing in the morning at Ronald McDonald House. Thank goodness Clyde didn't go home. Doctors rushing Todd back to St Paul in an ambulance — they think he is having seizures and they don't know what is causing it. Doctors keep saying blood gases OK. I've heard it till I could scream. I said I don't care, I care about Todd; please make him comfortable so he won't twist his neck out of line! Finally doctor comes and gets Todd comfortable and he is sleeping.

EXCERPT FROM TERRY'S DIARY

Tests revealed nothing. Todd's eye sight returned, but he was unable to eat and became very discouraged. He had no feeling from his chin to his toes so he could not help the doctors and staff with their diagnosis. So back to Dallas Rehab.

The doctors and staff at Dallas Rehab began to lose patience with Todd thinking he was not trying. Todd was very frustrated — the pain a person feels normally in his body when he is hurting came through to Todd as a pounding in his head, this was caused by his blood pressure skyrocketing out of control.

Clyde and I began watching Todd closely. We became convinced he was really in trouble. One morning when I heard a nurse being especially short with Todd, I spoke up.

Todd...

"Listen, Todd is not a complainer. He doesn't say something's wrong when it's not." Holding my temper in check, I went on. "He has accepted his condition and he's dealing with it with the guts of a man. I don't know what's wrong with him, but I do know it's something."

> Wednesday, July 3rd
>
> Todd's ready to go back to Dallas Rehab. Ambulance picks him up at 12:30 everything goes well. Everything is hectic at DRI — seems like a 3 ring circus in comparison to St Paul. We go back to Ronald McDonald's feeling very confident everything's OK! Took a nap went to the grocery store very relaxed. Went back at 4:30 to DRI, Todd's having more problems with breathing. Wilma the Resident Nurse is not giving him the treatment like Todd feels it should be (he's usually right) even Charles (is the aid and he loves Todd) is a little cross with Todd. Finally get him calmed down — had a pretty good night.

EXCERPT FROM TERRY'S DIARY

They must have believed me. The next thing I knew, they were running a CAT scan. The tests showed Todd had some brain injury. He had been having seizures, and while the doctors were saying, "You've got to straighten up and behave," Todd's brain was telling him he was not getting enough oxygen. It was an eerily similar situation to what had happened before at Baylor, but at least the staff at Dallas Rehab listened to us and reacted quickly to find the problem.

Since Todd was paralyzed from the chin down, his body did not react to the seizures as a normal person's would, so the staff could not visually recognize his symptoms. Todd was immediately put on Dilantin, a drug for the treatment of seizures. And when he started responding to it, I was able to relax a little.

It was a scary time. During those five days at the end of June and the beginning of July, Todd and I had gone back and forth from Dallas Rehab to St. Paul and back so many times, I lost count.

> **Thursday July 4th**
>
> Happy Holiday! Ha! First thing this morning phone call — didn't really excite me but come to find out it's DRI — they're taking Todd back to St Paul — blood in his lungs. May be just something minor — will run test and come back right back to DRI. Wrong! We now have a blood clot on the right side of the lung and he is readmitted to St Paul — will be here probably a week! We have a wonderful view. We're going to pull Todd's bed up the window and let him watch the fireworks.
>
> **Friday July 5th**
>
> Another crisis. Todd's had another bad night. They took him to x-ray and found not only the clot in his lung but 4 more, two in his groin and one in the lower leg. The doctors said surgery was needed to insert a balloon in his main aorta to catch any more clots before they hit his lungs. He could die if this happens.

EXCERPT FROM TERRY'S DIARY

Todd began to make progress with therapy, and Clyde made plans to go home. We needed the money so we could afford to keep Todd at Dallas Rehab. It was costing approximately $30,000 per month to keep him there. Our insurance would only cover a portion of that — it was up to us to pay the rest.

As the days passed, Todd was in therapy most of the day, and Clyde was home. That left me alone with my thoughts. One day, feeling a little homesick, I decided to visit my mother.

On the way to her house, I passed the big building that houses the Dallas Cowboys' offices. I felt a pang remembering Todd's dream of one

Todd...

day playing football for them. Suddenly, a wild idea hit me. I turned my car around and parked near the building. I didn't know what I was going to do, or who I should see, but I knew I had to do this thing for Todd, and for me.

"May I help you?" a pretty young receptionist asked, when I had found the Cowboy's front office. She sat motionless while I told her Todd's story and how his dream of being a Cowboy had been snuffed out by a diving accident.

MANY OF THE DALLAS COWBOY CHEERLEADERS CAME TO SEE TODD AND THEY GAVE HIM AN AUTOGRAPHED PICTURE WHICH WE PUT ON HIS "PHOTO WALL". (LATER ON I FRAMED IT AND IT WAS IN HIS BEDROOM. STACY HAS IT NOW. A REALLY GOOD MEMORY FOR BOTH OF US.)

"I wish someone here could go see him," I said.

Her face softened as she looked at the picture I handed her.

"It would help cheer him up," I went on. "He needs something to look forward to."

"He's a handsome boy — I'll see what I can do," she murmured with misty eyes.

I was overjoyed!

The following days were exciting. Most of the Dallas Cowboy Cheerleaders came to see Todd. I was thrilled as I watched his reactions (unmistakably male). The Cheerleaders encouraged him, telling him how handsome he was, promising to pray for him. Todd was proud of the autographed picture they gave him, and the Christian literature Coach Tom Landry sent.

The attention Todd was getting at this time encouraged me. I felt we desperately needed people, and their visits made me feel they really cared. But soon visitors became rare. Clyde's open hostility made it clear he didn't want anyone around.

The past two months had taken a toll on our family. Clyde was not really making that many trips back and forth — which was good for him because he was able to work and be with his friends — but it was very bad for me because I ended up spending a lot of time alone. My thoughts began to wonder if my husband was actually really working all the time he said he was. After all of the affairs Clyde had throughout our shaky marriage, it really didn't take a lot of imagination on my part to wonder what he was up to now.

Clyde was at our home near Emory and I was almost two hours away at Dallas Rehab with our son. I really needed his strength to help our family through this tumultuous time. I was very alone and very lonely. I needed his strength and I needed him to be with me.

A plan began forming in my mind. Clyde had always hated the lack of privacy at Ronald McDonald House. I decided that if we could get a place of our own nearby, he could stay with me and Stacy and commute to work. Then he would also be able to see Todd a lot more than he was able to being at home. So Stacy and I set out to find a place. I was very excited when we finally found a furnished apartment with a short term lease only minutes from Dallas Rehab. I could hardly wait to show it to Clyde.

"It's completely furnished, honey," I bubbled. "Even the dishes and linens. All we need are groceries."

Clyde agreed that it would be nice to have a place so close to Dallas Rehab, one even closer than Ronald McDonald House. So we rented the apartment, and I began my life away from home.

Clyde, however, only spent one night in the apartment during the months we had it. Stacy and I spent most of the time there alone.

Except for Stacy and me and the Dallas Rehab staff, Todd spent most of his time alone, too. It was summer, and his friends in Emory were busy doing their thing. It was a two hour trip — a little far for young people to drive alone.

There was a young girl, Toni Quizar, a precious young friend of Todd's who came a few times and sent cards and letters to encourage him. I didn't know that Toni had fallen in love with Todd their freshman year, so I didn't put two and two together. The days and nights were long for Todd, and for Stacy and me. Visitors meant a lot during that lonely time.

"If only I could get Todd out of here," I complained to Clyde on one of his Dallas Rehab visits. "When he's strong enough we could take him to our apartment. But we need a van," I added, hopefully.

"We don't need a van," Clyde responded. "He's not coming home in a wheel chair." Clyde still clung to the hope Todd would walk out of there.

Determined my plan would work, I began in my extra time to look for a van that could be converted into a handicap vehicle. Clyde was gone so much of the time now that I took it on myself to trade one of our cars in on it. Then I began the process of taking it to the people who would install the lifts and the handicap apparatus that would enable me to transport Todd. It was almost a month before it was ready.

By this time Todd was out of intensive care and in a regular room at Dallas Rehab, but he was still plagued with one thing after another. Kidney infection after kidney infection interfered with his therapy. Then he became malnourished which kept his neck from healing. The staff became irritated with him because he wouldn't eat. His weight had come down from two

MY SON

[TAKEN ABOUT 3 WEEKS BEFORE THE ACCIDENT]

TODD, AS A FRESHMAN, WAS HAVING A GREAT YEAR. VARSITY FOOTBALL PLAYER, NEW TRUCK FOR HIS BIRTHDAY. EVERYTHING SEEMED TO BE GOING HIS WAY. HIS DREAM OF BEING A PROFESSIONAL FOOTBALL PLAYER SEEMED VERY OBTAINABLE TO ALL OF US.

hundred eighty-eight pounds to two hundred thirty. They threatened to put a tube down his nose, but Todd was adamant.

"No way! They're not putting a tube down my nose!"

But, when Stacy and I arrived the next morning, a feeding tube was in Todd's nose. He was being fed a high-calorie, high-vitamin liquid. It looked like a malt.

"It sure don't taste like a malt," Todd complained, wriggling his nose disgustedly.

We learned he had put up such a fight when the tube was inserted, it took six people to hold him. Todd was paralyzed from the neck down, so all he could move was his head, but he had fought them with the strength of a bull. The tube stayed in two days before he managed to get it out. He begged the staff not to put it in again.

"Todd, we're all trying to help you," I said, impatiently. "Will you drink it on your own?"

With a defeated look, he agreed. It was then that I realized that he really was not anxious to live. His nutritional level had become so low that he was mentally and physically drained.

It took quite a while for Todd to begin to respond to the liquid he was drinking, but finally he began feeling better and gained some of his weight back. When the day came when he could actually come with us to our apartment, I was thrilled.

Now, if I can get my whole family together in our own apartment — everything will be all right, I thought.

Clyde was there with Stacy and me when we loaded Todd into the converted van. Todd was in his usual reclining position among the pillows in his wheelchair. I wanted so much to see him sitting up straight. Well, first things first.

I chattered away, ignoring the subdued atmosphere in the van. I was determined to make this day work, but Todd's visit did not turn out as I had pictured it. We talked a little, and even managed to laugh a little as I cooked dinner, but Todd slept most of the time.

Clyde was slowly realizing his son would never walk again. He would never play ball again or do any of the things Clyde wanted him to. That was a sad day for Clyde, but I had new hope for Todd. Maybe he would never get out of that chair, but I believed one day Todd would be happy again. He could only stay away from Dallas Rehab a couple of hours that first day and it was soon time for him to go back. The time had been too short.

At Dallas Rehab, Todd began to respond to therapy, and soon was weaned from the ventilator — something they thought would never happen. Things were beginning to really look better for our family — except for my relationship with my husband. Clyde was getting more and more despondent. He seemed angry much of the time and we were becoming more and more distant with each other.

It seemed the stronger I got, the more hostile Clyde became. One day when Clyde was leaving after visiting Todd, I walked with him to his pick-up.

"Honey, come to the apartment with me, please."

I just needed to be alone with him. I wanted him to hold me and tell me everything was all right, but my pleading did not move him. It was as if we were strangers.

"You're just being selfish, Terry." Clyde muttered, "You know I have to make a living — somebody's got to work. You can't complain when all you have to do is stay here and look after Todd. I don't think that's asking too much of you." He took a step away from me. "It's your responsibility to take care of Todd."

I had sold my Merle Norman store in Terrell which I had financed myself, so there was not a lot of money coming in from that. My other store in Quinlan was brand new and I had to hire a friend of mine to cover the store while I was with Todd. At the first of each month, Clyde and I had to come up with over $30,000 to keep Todd at Dallas Rehab. Yes, we needed money coming in. And, yes, Clyde needed to work. And our family also needed to be together. But it really hurt that Clyde seemed to be putting all of Todd's care on me with the excuse that only he was bringing an income into our family.

My heart ached as I watched the pick-up pull away. Clyde lit a cigarette and casually waved his hand as he drove away. I cried myself to sleep that night, on a pillow hugged tight in my arms.

The next days passed in a regular routine. Early mornings spent with Todd before therapy, lunch with Todd, and evenings after therapy with Todd. In between, I tried to remember I also had a daughter who needed me.

My daughter Stacy was so special, never complaining, and sometimes I couldn't help but feel guilty.

"It's okay, Mama, I love Todd, too. I want to help him get better," Stacy kept reassuring me.

STACY (ON RIGHT) WITH HER FRIEND SANDY.
AT THE TIME OF TODD'S ACCIDENT, STACY WAS ONLY 14 — SHE WOULD HAVE TO GROW UP VERY QUICKLY AND TOOK ON MANY ADULT RESPONSIBILITIES THAT SHE SHOULD NOT HAVE HAD TO. I DON'T KNOW WHAT I WOULD HAVE DONE WITHOUT HER STRENGTH.
SHE WAS MY ROCK.

CHAPTER 7
4 MONTHS — SMALL HOPE AMID A LARGER PAIN

There were times I was allowed to watch Todd in therapy. My feelings were mixed. It was wonderful to see someone else get better and walk out, but it was hard to never see any movement in Todd's body, until one day, Todd, with a mischievous glint in his eyes, asked me to go to therapy with him. The therapist placed Todd on the mat and put him through the range of motions as usual.

"Watch!" the therapist said.

Todd was trying to lift his left arm. I screamed excitedly and everyone laughed.

"I knew you'd do that," Todd said irritably. "I didn't really want to tell you because I knew you'd embarrass me."

"Todd, for goodness sake," I protested. "Think what this means." I was very excited. If Todd could just get to the point that he could maneuver his own chair — .

Back in my apartment that night I called all my family. Excitedly, I told them all he was doing. There had not been any movement, just a slight flinch, but after so long with no change (it had been sixteen weeks since Todd's accident), I was beside myself.

Todd was such a big handsome young man, and I tried to make him look his best, but he would not cooperate.

"I wish you'd leave me alone," he'd gripe when I washed his hair or put him in a new jogging suit.

The big wheelchair Dallas Rehab put Todd in made him look ugly. His feet were always up, and he reclined on pillows, but I'd wrestle him to an almost sitting position so he could be seen in his chair. All he wanted to do was sleep. However, therapy did help his attitude. The therapists would talk as they worked, encouraging and praising him. He really enjoyed therapy and looked forward to it. One therapist in particular caused his eyes to light up. She was cute, and Todd had noticed.

Dallas Rehab provided outings for their patients, so Todd and I decided to go with them to a movie one night. He rode in the van with me, and we stopped to eat at a restaurant before the movie. I wanted Todd to look as normal as possible, so when I fed him, I would give him a bite then I would take a bite, rather than feeding him as if he were an invalid. I was relieved when Todd didn't seem embarrassed.

Everything was going well until, during the movie, I was suddenly overcome with a feeling of discouragement. Todd's chair was huge. It was a manual chair, not an electric one. He had to have a lot of pillows to prop him up and he just looked awful. I wanted to see him scooting around like some of the other quads at Dallas Rehab, but instead he looked like Baby Huey — I hated it.

It had been only a month since he couldn't eat at all, now he ate everything in sight. His weight was coming back up too fast, and it was not only bad for him, it also made him look so much worse. Clyde thought Todd should eat anything he wanted — I felt he should eat healthier.

I was still depressed when the movie was over and we were on our way back to Rehab. I wanted Todd to take more pride in how he looked. I wanted people when they saw him to see the real Todd, not someone with a handicap. I was so upset on my way back to the apartment, my anger soon turned into tears.

The next morning I got to Dallas Rehab early and went straight to the dietitian to talk with her about Todd's diet.

"I know you have guidelines for the patients in what they eat, why aren't you enforcing them?" I demanded.

"We do have guidelines, but Todd won't cooperate," she responded.

"You're telling me that he won't cooperate?" I argued. "You have a captive audience there." Trying to calm down, I added, "I'll help anyway I can, but I want to see some results. I want some weight coming off Todd." As I was leaving, I added.

"And I want to see him sitting straight in his chair, who do I see about that? I want him to look like he's getting well instead of looking like a big blob lying in his chair."

I was crying by then, and I'm sure she thought I was crazy, but I didn't care. I just wanted Todd to look normal. After all, it was almost the end of the summer — how long does it take?

The dietitian sent me to see the occupational therapist, and in spite of my tears, I angrily explained what I wanted. I was determined Todd was going to shape up.

"It's been three months, when will he start looking like the other quads here? When will he sit up in his chair without all those pillows around him and without his feet propped up?"

If I couldn't get Todd to want to look better, I'd get to him through these people.

"It'll take time," the therapist said. "But he'll get there."

This was probably the turning point in Todd's mental recovery, the time when he accepted the reality of his condition. But the more Todd and I accepted his disability, the more distant Clyde became, and the more Clyde and I argued.

I realized something was wrong. Clyde had been unfaithful to me in the past, and I sensed it was happening again. I was heartsick, but surely it couldn't be true, not now — especially not now.

Since Todd's accident, I seldom went back to our home, but, now I felt the need to go. Clyde's mother had been house sitting for us while we stayed with Todd and was staying on since Clyde had gone back to work.

I took care of some things at home and was getting ready to leave for the hospital when the phone rang. It was a friend of mine who used to work for me when I still owned the Merle Norman Studio in Terrell, Texas. Judy had kept in touch with us to hear how Todd was doing. She was crying, and asked to speak to Clyde. She was surprised, and seemed a little flustered when she recognized my voice.

"Clyde isn't here, Judy," I said. "But can I help you?"

"Uh, well, I just got fired from my job and I was hoping maybe Clyde could give me a job in his store," Judy sniffled. "Just tell him I called."

That's strange, I thought as I hung up the phone. But I put it in the back of my mind as I drove back to the Dallas Rehab Center. Several days later, Clyde called me at the apartment.

"Terry, I need our birth certificates. Where are they?" He seemed frantic.

"Why do you need our birth certificates?" I asked.

"I'm taking out more life insurance on myself in case anything happens to me — so you and the kids will be taken care of," Clyde mumbled.

I was puzzled, but I told him where the certificates were. This wasn't like Clyde. It seemed odd, especially with everything going on in our lives right now, that he would be thinking about life insurance. For some strange reason, Judy's phone call came to my mind, and also the way Clyde had been acting lately. I started drawing a very uncomfortable conclusion.

I put my suspicions on hold because of my concern for Todd. I felt that he was not progressing in his therapy as well as he should. Six months is the time usually allotted for a case such as Todd's, but by now he'd been there four months already and things were not coming together as I thought they should. The doctors had also said he had developed a prostate problem and at some point in the near future, they would have to operate to correct it.

Although Clyde knew about Todd's recent setback, he informed me that he had to go out of town on business and would be gone a week. I shrugged it off and made up my mind to get through everything the best I could.

While Clyde was gone, the situation with Todd became an emergency, and once again he was rushed, red lights flashing, back to St. Paul Hospital for emergency surgery. We tried to contact Clyde, but couldn't find him. Todd was petrified to go through the operation without his dad with him.

Thoughts about the birth certificates kept fluttering through my mind. I allowed my imagination free reign and pictured Clyde and Judy in the Bahamas or in Mexico. *Probably Mexico,* I thought. We were in the Bahamas a year before and he'd want to take her somewhere different.

Todd wanted his dad with him. The only way I had to get through to him was through the guys who worked for him! All they would say is that they would get a message from me to him – but he couldn't come home right then. (I found out later that he was truly in Cancun, Mexico with Judy for a week's vacation.) Clyde's employees did get in touch with him and his reply was very nonchalant.

"I can't come home right now," was all he bothered to say.

Todd came through the prostate surgery very well. This time I decided that since Clyde was on his "outing," the kids and I might as well be comfortable — so Stacy and I stayed in a suite adjoining Todd's room while he recuperated.

Why not, I thought resentfully. *We need to be comfortable for a change.*

As I lay in my bed at night I'd see Clyde and Judy in Mexico, probably Cancun. Judy loved Cancun… A nice hideaway where she would love to be with my husband.

Judy was very attractive and I had always wished I could be like her. Now, all I could think of was her bleached blond hair next to my husband and it hurt as I pictured them together.

Todd had been in the hospital a week when Clyde stuck his head through the door to Todd's room.

"What happened? What's going on?" He asked innocently. "I didn't know anything about this."

"We tried to call you," I said, trying for Todd's sake to keep my feelings in check.

As I listened to his excuses, I had the most gut-sick feeling of my entire life. That was a hard day. I had to act naturally when all I wanted to do was scream. I didn't want to upset Todd so I kept my feelings to myself.

Clyde said he would pick up something for our dinner that night, and I decided to go with him. When I opened the pick-up door and looked inside, I knew Judy had been there. Clyde's pick-up was neat as a pin. Judy had always been a cleaning fanatic, and the truck was immaculate. There was even a brand new beer cooler.

That's for their drinks, I thought with a pang in my stomach. I knew I had to stop these thoughts and outwardly, I just passed my attitude off as my worry about Todd. I felt that Clyde sensed that I knew he was seeing someone, but he was trying to act normal. When he reached out to pat my knee, I flinched involuntarily.

"What's wrong with you, Terry?" He asked, slowing the truck at a traffic light. "I can't help it if I have to work. You know I'd rather have been here with Todd."

I suspected he was using anger to try to put guilt on me so he would be off the hook.

The fact that I didn't really know that anything was going on between Clyde and Judy did cause a twinge of guilt to find its way into my conscience. I wanted to believe nothing was going on. I loved this man so much, and I had poured so much of my life into him and my family through the years. For twenty-three years I had tried to give him the benefit of the doubt, but now... Oh surely, he wouldn't be doing anything like that now anyway, not when his son's very life was at stake.

I decided to just put the whole situation aside and not rock the boat. I wasn't emotionally capable of handling any marriage problems right then, but I knew that I might have to face some pretty hard choices down the road.

BIRTHDAY SHENANIGANS WITH TODD, CLYDE AND ME

CHAPTER 8
5 MONTHS — WELCOME HOME

When Todd was able, he was transported, once again by ambulance, back to Dallas Rehab Center, back to therapy, and we were back to watching for any sign of improvement.

There was no movement in Todd's body, and it looked like this was the way it would always be. He would be able to use only the sip and puff chair — one that Todd could use his mouth to maneuver. In spite of this, Todd's attitude was improving, and so was his health. He was smiling more and more. And he could leave Rehab for short outings in the evening if it wasn't his shower night.

Todd's new improved attitude was put to the test a few days later. My mother invited Todd and me to have dinner with her. However, once we got there, we couldn't get Todd up the steps into her house. We hadn't thought about needing a ramp, and even so, his chair wouldn't have fit through the door. We tried the patio, but found that we couldn't get the chair up the one step.

Defeated, we ended up eating on Mother's carport. We tried to have fun for my mother's sake, but it was pretty depressing for Todd and me. That was our first encounter with the problem of inaccessibility for the handicapped.

When Todd was in the van, he could only sit facing the side rather than the front as his size would only allow us to back his wheel chair straight into the van off the lift. So when we were riding together, I could look at him through the rear view mirror and see his face.

That day as Todd and I pulled out of Mother's driveway, I heard a deep sigh from the back. I glanced in the mirror as Todd sighed again.

"Mama, I just wish I could have fun again."

I didn't comment right away. *Oh, Jesus,* I thought. *What do I say to him?* I searched for an encouraging word.

"Todd, what is fun?"

Todd sighed again.

"I don't know, what is it?"

"I believe fun is more mental than anything." I replied. "Todd," I swallowed the tears that threatened. "Fun can be watching the sun go down, or watching the birds in the trees, listening to music. It's whatever you make it. Todd, there are many people in the world who have two good arms and two good legs, but they are more paralyzed than you because they don't know how to enjoy life."

I watched his head tilt as he listened intently.

"Honey, whether you are in that chair, or walking around on two good legs, you have to make the choice to be happy. No one can do that for you. And that is the only way you will get through this new way of life." I glanced quickly over my shoulder at Todd. "Do you understand?"

"Yeah, I guess."

Todd was accepting his condition much better than I could have. And, according to many others, better than they. Several said they would rather die than to have to live like that, but my Todd seemed to have made the decision that he wanted to live, no matter what. It appeared that he had finally accepted the challenge.

It was not only a challenge for Todd, but for me, too. Taking care of Todd was trying both emotionally and physically on me. I had to manually roll his chair onto the lift when I took him anywhere in the van. Todd now weighed about two hundred forty pounds, so he and the heavy chair were quite a load. It was a wrestling match — but it was worth it to get Todd out into the world. I knew this was only the beginning of the struggle if I was going to take care of Todd at home. But right then, we had to take one day at a time.

Once we had gotten over the initial breathing problem at Dallas Rehab (that Todd was really having seizures and could not breathe) and the staff realized that Todd was not either misbehaving or not trying, everyone came to love him because he had now become a hero. They really could see what a normally optimistic and good natured personality he had. We all had to just get beyond that first crisis so that everyone at Dallas Rehab could learn to love him, and then they had sort of "adopted me" because I was there most of the time.

I had never been an over-protective mother, but now I felt that I should be there for Todd all the time. We had to manage by ourselves since his dad rarely came to see him anymore.

Stacy had gone back home and was staying with her grandmother. It was almost time for school to start, and she had to buy school clothes without me. She was forced to take responsibility for herself, and had to grow up too fast. She came up on weekends, but I missed having her to talk to, and I just missed having a familiar face nearby. But Todd and I were learning to cope and things were becoming fairly routine.

Todd was able to sit up better and we decided it was time for us to go home for a visit. The prospect of going home, even for a short time, was exciting, but I had to be trained to take care of all of Todd's needs. I was taught how to take care of his bladder program and how to bathe and dress him. I hadn't seen Todd's body since he was a little boy and had learned to take care of himself, but there was no room for modesty or shyness and soon I was able to roll up my sleeves and do it all.

I also had to be prepared for emergency situations — I learned to use the Ambu bag, an apparatus for giving Todd oxygen if he had a problem breathing. I did all right, and we were soon ready to go home for an overnight visit.

Stacy and I wanted to give Todd a welcome home party, but Clyde didn't think giving Todd a party was a good idea. It had been almost five months since Todd had been home, and I felt he needed to get on with his life. The kids he went to school with wanted to see him, so what better way than a welcome home party? So I just ignored Clyde's argument.

Stacy announced the welcome home party over the loud speaker at school, telling everyone that Todd would be home that Saturday about mid-day.

I made a quick trip home so I could help get things ready for the party. Stacy, Clyde's sister and her husband and I got everything ready for what we hoped would be a fantastic party for Todd. We made streamers and posters and banners with slogans welcoming Todd home.

Then I set about getting Todd to look as good as he possibly could. Even though he was in a wheelchair, I wanted him to portray the personality that was Todd, and for his friends to think of him as being as normal as possible.

I did have a little trouble with his hair. All the medication he had taken had turned his hair a dark, coarse, unhealthy brown, so I used a lightener on it, hoping it would look more normal. When I finished however, his hair had turned a light, coarse, and unhealthy looking orange. It didn't help Todd's attitude any and did help precipitate a terrible argument about the trip home.

"Todd, I want to tell you something," I cried, wiping tears away impatiently. "I suffered death bringing you into this world and the least you can do is let me do this." I was a little ashamed of myself for using guilt but I knew seeing his friends would be good for him.

"I just want a simple trip home, Mama," Todd grumbled, "I don't want a big deal made out of it."

Todd had never had a problem with self-esteem, but I think he felt a little apprehensive, a little scared of what his classmates would think of him. But, when the time came, and as I dressed him and he saw how good he looked, he was as excited as I was. We just put a cap on his orange hair and he was all set. But by the time we got half way home, I was beginning to have second thoughts. Maybe Clyde was right. I had been wrong before about letting his friends see him. *What if this sets Todd back?* I thought anxiously.

When we came in sight of the house, I was awestruck.

"Oh, my gosh! Todd, you are not going to believe this," I said.

Cars were lined up all the way to the highway and our huge yard was filled with cars and kids. Todd was facing away from the house so he couldn't see until I turned into the long drive. A big grin flashed across his disbelieving face. I knew he wanted, with all his being, to just throw the door of the van open and run to meet his friends, but with patience, possessed only because of the invisible bands holding him helpless, he waited for me to let the lift down and maneuver his chair onto familiar ground.

The kids who had been eagerly waiting for us, now stood back in hushed silence, watching this guy who had left, a football lineman, coming back completely helpless and dependent on someone else for his every move. The strain the kids were feeling showed on each of their young faces as they stood not knowing what to do next.

"Kids, come on over and say hi to Todd," I shouted.

I was more nervous than I had ever been, but I felt that Todd's future was at stake. Todd, shy before all his guests, kept his sip and puff straw* in his mouth, and it was up to me to welcome them. Standing by my son's wheelchair in the hot Texas sun, I coaxed his friends toward us.

Tentatively, one-by-one they came forward and I moved aside as a small crowd gathered around Todd — his obvious acceptance of his situation began to ease the tension. I stood back in amazement realizing the courage it must be taking for my son to handle this reunion, and for the kids as they reached out to Todd — willing to make allowances for any limitations.

During the party, the Wildcat's head coach made his way through the crowd until he was standing beside me where I was pouring yet another glass of lemonade.

"Mrs. Odom," Coach Brenham cleared his throat. "Friday is homecoming, and we wondered if, maybe, you could bring Todd back so he could be with us." With a glint of tears in his eyes he went on. "We realize, if Todd hadn't had the accident, he'd be in the lineup."

I tried to control the grin on my face, as I quickly said,

"I'm sure that can be arranged. We'll have to check with Dallas Rehab to see if he can come home again next weekend, but I know we can pull it off."

Football had been the hardest thing for Todd, and us, to give up. Being so big had limited his participation in most sports, but he had finally found his niche... *in football.*

The party ended after a couple of hours. Todd was tired.

Even though the atmosphere had been a little subdued, it was clear

---

If a quad gets no movement back — they use a "sip and puff" wheel chair — that means it is maneuvered by blowing to go forward and sipping to make it go backwards. Todd was a very good "puffer" and "sipper."

everyone was glad Todd was back. Their relationship would be easier when he was home for good.

The party had been a good thing. Todd was on his way home.

TODD'S FIRST TRIP HOME – FACING HIS FRIENDS AND HIS NEW LIFE
HE STILL HAS 3 MORE MONTHS OF REHAB TO GO

CHAPTER 9
WHEN REALITY SETS IN

There had been only one cloud over an otherwise perfect homecoming day for Todd — Clyde had waited until late that afternoon to show up, and then only stayed a short while saying he had to get back to work. (I was tired of keeping up this farce we called a marriage. It was getting easier and easier for me to think of separation.)

Our house had not yet been remodeled to accommodate Todd's chair. Todd couldn't even get into his room, so he slept in mine. He seemed more secure when I was near him at night anyway, and it worked out well — at least for this short visit.

That Sunday evening Todd had to be back at Dallas Rehab at eight forty-five p.m. We spent the day enjoying being home and planning things we would do when we were both home for good.

Back at Dallas Rehab, Todd was still excited and very upbeat as we got back into the routine of therapy — knowing he would be with his team Friday, even if he wouldn't be playing. His coach had given him a jersey with his old number to wear in the lineup so he would feel more a part of the team. (Of course I wanted him to wear the pads, as well.)

"Aw, Mom!" Todd said with exasperation. (And didn't.)

Friday, as I pulled the jersey over Todd's head, I thought my heart would explode with the joy I felt knowing that he was accepted and welcomed as a member of a team on which we knew he'd never play.

Clyde came to Dallas to be with Todd for the two hour trip back home. I drove the van and Todd sat behind me. Normally, his dad would have sat in the front with me — this time he sat in the very back of the van.

"I'll just sit back here with Todd, okay?" he said casually.

Todd...

I burned with anger. It was sure okay with me. I had heard that he and Judy were living together and if I had any doubts before about who his new girlfriend was, that trip convinced me.

Todd and Clyde talked about the game ahead. I just listened, disappointed that this could not also be a happy time for Clyde and me. We were nearly home when I glanced in the rearview mirror and saw Clyde take something from his shirt pocket.

"Look what I got Mamaw," he said to Todd.

I saw a sparkle in the mirror as he went on.

"I thought she might like these earrings." He tilted them toward me when he saw that I was looking in the mirror.

"You like 'em, Terry?"

I was right, I thought. *It really is Judy.* I knew Clyde Odom would never have bought diamond stud earrings for his mother. This was Judy's handiwork.

When the van stopped. I got out and pushed the buttons for the doors to swing open on the van and the lift came down ready for Todd to disembark. This time rather than me pushing him,* it was Clyde who took the role of getting him placed just right so that I could then lower the lift. I reengaged the chair for Todd and off he went into the house. Mamaw and Stacy were there along with some others of our family — it seemed like another party. But it was the anticipation of the football game ahead that really made the day exciting.

We were ready to leave for the game when Clyde called me into our bedroom. Turning to me he said,

"Something's wrong with my contact lens. I think I have something in my eye. See if you can fix it."

Clyde had never quite been able to do that for himself, so I checked it out. As I cleaned the lens, I realized I just wanted him to go away. I just didn't want to worry anymore about what he was doing, or where he was going, or what was going on in his life. As I returned the lens to his eye, I calmly said,

---

He was still in the sip and puff wheel chair which had to be disengaged and manually pushed in order to get him on or off the lift.

"You're going to have to teach Judy to do this, because this is the last time I'll do it for you."

A look of disbelief crossed Clyde's face. He now knew that I knew. He didn't ask how I found out, and he must have heard something in my voice that told him it would do no good to deny it. But, I didn't have time to worry about Clyde and Judy — I had to focus all my energy on Todd at this point and had no time to worry about what his daddy was doing or who he was doing it with.

Clyde had been happy and excited when we got home, but when we left for the stadium he seemed to be preoccupied and depressed. The drive over to Emory took about twelve minutes — the longest, most uncomfortable twelve minutes I've ever been through. There was a little nervous chatter between Clyde and me, but he didn't have any problem at all talking football with Todd.

As I turned the corner going past the stadium, we got caught up in the commotion and excitement that always surrounds a ball game. Our windows were down and we could hear the sound of the band, the roar of the crowd. Someone saw our van, and then we heard on the PA system an announcement of Todd's arrival.

I forgot everything else. Once again, we went through what was becoming a routine processs of getting Todd out of the van. But the minute he was out and his wheel chair on the ground — he was gone. I stood by the van choked with emotion as I watched my son wheel out onto the running track that surrounded the football field. The crowd roaring, the lights, the band, and cheerleaders chanting, "Welcome home, Todd!"

"We'd like to welcome back Todd Odom," boomed the announcer's voice over the loud speaker. "He's going to be our honorary football captain for this evening. Todd has been in a rehabilitation center for the past five months, and we want to welcome him home, and we hope that he will be coming back to school soon. Welcome home, Todd!"

Then Todd rolled out onto the field in front of the stands.

My heart swelled with pride and I had to fight back tears of joy as I watched from the sidelines. Clyde and I stayed out of the way, but we were so grateful and so proud when we saw how the kids swarmed around Todd,

Todd...

talking to him and taking care of him. This was Todd's night, and his smile showed how glad he was to be in the middle of all this again, even in a wheelchair.

Later, during the game, I saw tears on Clyde's face, and I assumed they were for his son who was not on the field, but since he knew his affair with Judy was no longer a secret from me, he was probably facing some decisions he hadn't planned to face — at least not then.

After the game, Clyde, Stacy and I drove Todd back to Dallas Rehab. We didn't have permission to keep him overnight because of some medication he needed, but we intended to bring him back home Saturday.

Clyde was not spending the night with us. He had made his decision, and his choice was Judy.

"The only thing I ask," I said, "is that I would like us to keep it secret until we bring Todd home for good."

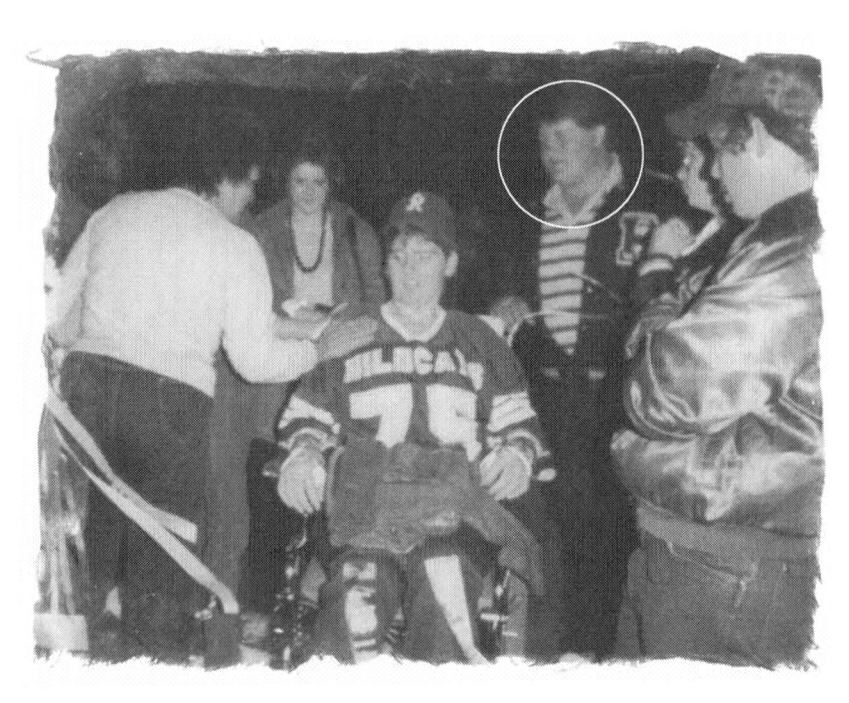

THIS WAS TODD'S NIGHT — AND HE WAS GLAD
TO BE IN THE MIDDLE OF IT ALL

The football player on Todd's left, Kendal (shown circled), had graduated the previous year. Todd would have taken his place on the varsity team.

It was important to me to keep up the pretense at Dallas Rehab of our being a happy family. Clyde agreed to keep pretending, then when we were home for good, we'd divorce.

I slept well that night for the first time in a long while. The game playing was finally over. This was different than the affairs he had had before. There were usually suspicions on my part, then, I would confront him and he'd drop the woman and come home to me. This time, Clyde said he was in love with Judy and wanted to make it "permanent".

Even though I felt better getting it over with, it still hurt. I could not understand how Clyde could choose to leave us now when we needed him more than ever. I had wanted to talk about Judy, but he put me off saying we could talk the next day.

Stacy and I were at Dallas Rehab early Saturday morning to pick Todd up. He was anxious to get back home. It was a joy for him to look forward to being in his own home after being gone for over five months. We headed back to our home for at least a weekend of a normal life.

According to our "friends," Clyde had been living a normal life — and having a great time all summer. While his family was in the midst of a nightmare, Clyde and Judy were skiing on Lake Ray Hubbard where they had rented a condo and vacationing in the Bahamas.

Todd was paralyzed and was going to stay paralyzed. The apple of his daddy's eye would never be that professional athlete Clyde dreamed he would be. My faith made me stronger and stronger, but Clyde had not made a commitment to the Lord, so he dealt with the situation the only way he knew, he ran in the opposite direction.

Clyde was home Saturday night long enough to put Todd to bed. I was completely worn out physically and emotionally. Again we put him in my bed because the wheelchair would not go in his room. That weekend was so wonderful because of Todd's homecoming, but it was also very draining for me.

Clyde and I fought about everything, especially how I took care of Todd. He thought I should give in to Todd's every whim, but, since I had to do it all, I felt I should do it the way I thought best.

I knew that weekend there would never be anything more between Clyde and me. I also knew I would have to give up my apartment in Dallas since I would no longer be able to afford it. From now on, I would have to make a new life for myself, too.

Back at Dallas Rehab Center, Todd went on with therapy. It had been five months since the accident and, to me, it looked like there would never be any change.

Then, one day Todd again asked me to come with him to his therapy session. The therapist took him out of his chair and laid him flat on his back on a mat. I watched, and on his left side, there was — ever so small — a trace of a muscle that was trying to lift his arm.

What this slight movement in his left forearm meant was that if this was truly movement coming back in the muscle — it could be strengthened and developed — which would mean he would not have to go home in a "sip and puff "wheelchair. He would be able to maneuver what's called a "joy stick," a lever on the left side of the arm of the chair. He would then be able to have a push and pull movement in his left arm that would allow him to be mobile and independent.

I squealed in surprised joy. This time Todd was not embarrassed. I had quit expecting any movement, and even though this was a small thing, it was something. Maybe later there would be more. Who knew what would be five years down the road?

Todd wanted his daddy to know, so I called him. Clyde and I had agreed that Judy should not come to Dallas Rehab because of the decision we made to pretend to be a family while we were there. We still spent time together there, but Clyde's visits to Todd were few.

Todd and I were to attend a seminar that afternoon at Dallas Rehab on how to take care of a quadriplegic. When I walked into Todd's room later on that day I noticed he had his dad's boots on. Then I saw lipstick on his cheek. Trying to sound casual, I asked,

"Who kissed you?"

"Nobody," he answered.

"Somebody did, because there's lipstick on you. Who kissed you, Todd?" I persisted.

"I can't tell you," he grinned.

"Todd, I want to know. Judy kissed you, didn't she?"

"How did you know? You know about Judy?" he asked.

"Yeah, I know about Judy."

"I didn't want to upset you, Mama."

I felt flushed with an anger that I could barely control. Todd and I went to the seminar but I couldn't concentrate.

"Todd, I can't sit here, I have some things to do." I excused myself and left. I was furious. *He couldn't even do this for me,* I thought angrily. *He couldn't even keep Judy away long enough for us to get Todd settled at home.* I felt humiliated and betrayed.

I drove 90 miles an hour to their condo. I had never interfered with their relationship, but if they had been home that day, I don't know what I would have done to them. They weren't. Out of control, I drove to a service station where I used a pay phone to call a friend, one of the guys who worked for Clyde. Mark Mullins listened as I tearfully unloaded my anger.

"This is nothing that you didn't expect, Terry," he reminded me. "That's just Clyde. That's just the way he is."

I knew he was right, and I calmed down.

"Thank you for listening, Mark," I said. "I really needed to talk to someone."

Rain battered my windshield as I drove back to Dallas Rehab. Todd and I had planned to go to the Texas State Fair when he was finished with his therapy that day, but because of the weather, we spent the afternoon talking about what was going on with his dad.

"Why didn't you tell me you knew about Judy, Mama?"

"The timing wasn't right, Todd," I answered. "I just didn't want you to have to face this yet."

Todd and I talked all evening. I was grateful that such a deep understanding had developed between us since his accident. After I left Dallas

Rehab, I felt such a loneliness, I decided to go home rather than stay at the apartment.

THE BRIDGE OVER LAKE TAWAKONI — WE HAD JUST MOVED FROM A BEAUTIFUL LITTLE LAKE HOUSE ON LAKE TAWAKONI TO JUST OUTSIDE EMORY ABOUT A YEAR BEFORE TODD'S ACCIDENT

OUR "BIG" HOUSE OUTSIDE EMORY, TX
THE "ONE FLOOR" LIVING AND SOME ADDITIONAL REMODELING MADE IT A PERFECT PLACE TO BRING TODD HOME AFTER HIS ACCIDENT

CHAPTER 10
TORN ASUNDER

We lived on Lake Tawakoni about a year before the accident. The lake is very, very large and there's a really long causeway and then a bridge crosses the center of the lake to some very exclusive properties. This is where Clyde, Todd, Stacy and I had lived as a family before the accident. Then one day, Stacy found what we called "the big house" and they talked me into buying and moving into this new house shortly before Todd's accident. I really loved our little house on Lake Tawakoni, but looking back, I can see God's hand even in this purchase. If I had held onto my little house on the lake, Todd would have not been able to come home there — his chair wouldn't have fit, we could not have made it handicapped accessible — my lovely little house would not have worked. So, at the time of his accident, we were firmly in our "big" house near Emory.

Whenever I traveled from "the big house," the interstate ran right by Lake Ray Hubbard — so, I think it's probably understandable that I was just a little upset that for some very strange and possibly insane reason, or just to make me crazy, Clyde and Judy chose a condo that was on the west side of Lake Ray Hubbard, one very visible from the interstate that crossed the bridge — the bridge I had to travel every single time I went to see our son.

So, every time I went from our home outside of Emory to Dallas Rehab, I had to pass by their condo. And every single time I made that trip, I was reminded that my husband's life seemed to be going back to something akin to "normal" while mine was still very much in a dilemma. It seemed as if Clyde could care less and less about me and our family — and living right there and being with my former friend Judy was just one more knife to stick in to make me crazy. Then I found out that Clyde and Judy had rented the condo over two months before I found out about their affair. I have to laugh now of all the times I passed by that condo before I actually knew that they were living right there. It's probably a very good thing for everyone that I didn't know.

But, on the day I found out Judy had come with Clyde to see Todd, and Clyde had once again broken a promise to me — I just had to find out for myself exactly what their setup was. *Now would be a good time to stop by Clyde's and Judy's apartment for a talk,* I thought. We could discuss the whole situation, get out into the open what I expected from them and what they expected out of me. So, going home from Dallas Rehab, I made the decision to go to their condo and find out just where I stood and how their plans for the future involved my family.

On the drive there, I felt calm and in control. I pulled into their driveway and there they were, unloading firewood from Clyde's pick-up. I was not prepared for the homey atmosphere, getting wood together, living together in a beautiful condo decorated by Judy with her usual perfection.

"Hello," I said, my voice shaking.

"Don't cause any trouble, Terry," Clyde warned me.

"I'm not here to cause trouble. I just want to talk."

Then my hurt came pouring out.

"How dare you! How dare you take her to Dallas Rehab when I asked you not to? I cannot believe you would do this to me."

"Well, I couldn't help it," Clyde defended himself. "Todd was doing so good, he looked so good when I went over there, I wanted to share it with Judy. I wanted her to see how well he was doing."

Our twenty-three years together did not seem to count for anything with Clyde anymore. This other woman was much more important to him than I was, or even his children.

"It's out in the open now, and what's done is done," he said.

I conceded the point. But we still needed some ground rules.

"If you and Judy are going to continue to go there, I think you should both get training to take care of Todd. If you're going to stay together, then you should both be trained so you can bring him home with you sometime.

I would like to have some weekends for me for a change." I only said that to cover my wounded heart. I didn't need any weekends. I didn't have any place to go anyway.

The rain was pouring as I left Clyde and Judy's. On the way home tears from emotions pent up for months poured unchecked down my cheeks. The hurt I felt made it hard to understand my husband's affair, but that he would do it at this time of anguish in his family's life was unbearable.

Mamaw, who had been staying at our house with Stacy, met me at the door when I reached home. Clyde had called and was very upset that I was not home yet. Mamaw and Stacy were worried because I was out in such bad weather. My mother-in-law and I talked late into the night. She was devastated. She felt, as I did, that Clyde could have at least helped us get through this time in our lives before leaving.

The financial support we needed from Clyde began to depend on whether my behavior suited him or not. He made it clear to me that he loved Judy and planned to marry her, and they were going to be happy. He also made it clear that he felt my job was to take care of Todd and make him happy. But I decided I was not going to just wither away — I was going to be happy, too.

It seemed to me we were in the middle of a cruel joke. Our son lay in the hospital completely paralyzed, and here Clyde and I were making the decision to break up a twenty-three year marriage. I didn't feel particularly depressed or unhappy. I knew it was time, but the timing was not great. I knew there was a struggle ahead for Todd. There would be a struggle ahead for me, too.

Bitterness tugged at my tired mind as I thought about Clyde. He was in control. I had no money. I had sold one of my stores, and it took all the profit from the other store just to keep it running. Clyde was the one who was working and he made it clear to me that I had no choice. I was expected to take care of Todd — which I would have done anyway, but to have someone hold a financial hammer over your head is very difficult to take.

Torn between wanting to take care of my son, and needing help physically and financially, I listed the things I felt I was entitled to out of the divorce, which only met with hostility from Clyde. He was in the driver's seat. I had no job, no money, and no time even, to fight him.

I had to give up the apartment in Dallas because Clyde would no longer pay the rent. Since I had no choice but to pack up and move home, it was necessary for me to commute to and from Dallas Rehab every day. I would leave home at nine a.m. and get back at eleven p.m. On the weekends I would bring Todd home.

This routine was made easier by Todd's friends who came over to visit on the weekends. Also, some of the guys who had worked for Clyde would come to our house to play cards with Todd and just be there to talk and help. Mark Mullins, in particular, became a true friend, someone we could depend on. I had no real close friends, and I needed someone other than Stacy to lean on. Mark became that someone. He just took us under his wing and was a friend for all of us.

There were so many things on my shoulders, it was wonderful to have someone I could turn to for help. Since we were planning on bringing Todd home for good very soon, major remodeling had to be done on our house to make it livable for him as he needed to be able to go anywhere in the house.

I didn't regret having to give up the apartment in Dallas because I enjoyed being home again — even with all the traveling back and forth to Dallas Rehab. It was mid-October, and I had not lived at home since May.

One beautiful morning I got up feeling like my old perky self. There were some things I wanted to do in the house. Some pictures and mirrors needed hanging, so I decided to go to Dallas Rehab in the afternoon.

I was puttering around the house when the door opened, and the familiar odor of Clyde's cigarettes drifted in. His tall, lanky body seemed to fill the room. He looked sad — an expression seldom seen on his face. We hadn't seen each other since the night I went by his and Judy's condo. I cynically wondered what was up.

Clyde was very nostalgic, and even seemed a little contrite. He was sorry our family was not together, and before he left he put his arms around me and said,

"I still love you, Terry, and I want to come home."

Shocked, I put down the familiar feeling of hope I felt, and backed away from him. How could he confuse me like this? How could he say the things he did just a month ago and now want to come home? I couldn't believe his audacity. No way was I going to uproot the life I was putting together for myself and my kids. I didn't even try to hold back the words.

"No way, you've made your bed, now you can lie in it."

But, as usual, Clyde was able to "talk me around." And when I left for Dallas Rehab to see Todd, it was with the feeling that maybe, just maybe, I would be back in Clyde's life and he in mine.

It was late when I got back from Dallas Rehab that night. As I pulled into the long drive I saw Mark's truck. I stopped beside him as he rolled his window down and said,

"Terry, I need to talk to you. I just wanted you to know that Clyde and Judy have been picked up."

"Picked up? Picked up for what?" I shook my head to clear the tired jumble of thoughts that clung to my mind like cobwebs. I was still reeling from Clyde's visit earlier, now this.

"They were caught in a drug lab cooking amphetamines and they're in jail down in East Texas," said Mark.

I couldn't believe it! *What now?* I thought. Clyde made a lot of money and I had begun to suspect how some of it was made — but now I was confronted with cold reality.

Clyde and Judy had been in jail three days when Clyde persuaded a trustee to call and ask me to go down to the jail. This was all beginning to make sense to me, now. I remembered Clyde's plea to come home. He knew he was already in trouble when he came to see me. I felt like throwing the phone against the wall. What kind of fool did he think I was?

The nudge I felt inside had a familiar touch — I felt that God was reminding me that Clyde was still my husband, and I needed to help him, no matter how I felt.

The following Sunday I drove the forty-five miles to the jail to visit Clyde. Listening to a tape of gospel songs on the way, I felt my heart begin to soften, and tears fell freely down my face. *Lord,* I thought, *Are you getting Clyde and me back together?* He's hurt me so much. My thoughts were tumbling over each other as I considered the possibility. (*Isn't it funny how women just hang on to the possibility of keeping their families together?*)

I felt embarrassed as I asked to see Clyde — it was humiliating. I watched as Clyde walked toward me in a room that was hardly any bigger than a closet, and take a seat behind a small glass partition that separated us. He fumbled for a cigarette but he held it unlit in a trembling hand as he reached for the phone.

I could see new lines in my husband's handsome face as he leaned toward the glass, blinking away tears. His subdued voice wavered as he gave me instructions on how to post bond. Then, holding me with his eyes, he said,

"Terry, I really do want to come home."

Feeling confused, I answered,

"Clyde, I'll do what you ask, but I won't be the one to get Judy out of jail. You'll have to do that yourself."

Clyde blinked, unused to me being firm with him.

"Okay," he agreed. "That's fine."

I had loved Clyde since I was thirteen years old, and from that time I had always done his bidding. It seemed to me that he had been my whole life, but things were different now.

For three days I worked on getting Clyde released, but when his lawyer showed me the papers I was to sign on the three pieces of land Clyde was using for collateral, I balked. Judy's name was on all three. Clyde had promised Judy would not be involved in this, but not knowing what else to do, I reluctantly signed. I felt like such a fool.

Then I was faced with having to make a two trip from Dallas to Gilmer, Texas to get them out of jail and bring them back to Dallas to the bondman. I kept thinking, *I'm such a fool!* I was halfway there before I realized how crazy this was —why on earth was I going to get my husband and his girlfriend out of jail? I couldn't do it. I wouldn't do it. Furious with myself for even starting on the trip, I called Mark Mullins and asked him to meet me in Canton and bring along someone who could drive me back to Emory. Mark would then go on to Gilmer, pick up Clyde and Judy, and drive them back to Dallas. There was no way I could face Clyde or Judy right then. And why should I?

So, Mark picked Clyde and Judy up in my car and brought them back to Dallas. Clyde promised me he and I would talk the next morning. I wanted to know exactly what had been going on, why they had been arrested, and what was going to happen next.

After a sleepless night, I waited for Clyde to call, but seven a.m. came, then eight, and no call — I called their condo. Judy answered. Clyde wasn't up, but she handed him the phone.

"You promised we could talk this morning, Clyde," I said accusingly.

"I'll come over later," Clyde said in a level voice.

"What time?" I persisted.

"About eleven or twelve," he said not bothering to hide his irritation and impatience from me.

Eleven o'clock came and went, then twelve o'clock and he hadn't come. I had done everything he had asked me to do, all the running around, all that paper work. Finally, I realized he had once again made a fool of me. I didn't know if I was more disgusted with Clyde or myself. I decided to just go back to Dallas Rehab.

As I drove, my imagination was in overdrive. I pictured myself meeting them on the highway, and I wondered what I would do. I remembered stories of people who had done awful things because they had gone temporarily insane. I felt hysteria rising in me and I felt I could be capable of anything at this point. *I've been tricked,* I thought as I remembered the things I had done for them. Not only did I get them out of jail, I had loaned them Todd's van — Judy's car and Clyde's pick-up had been confiscated by the narcotics officers. They were having a good time at my expense. I half hoped I really would meet them on the road. Picturing it in my mind... I'd go for Judy first. I'd pull her out of that van and...

Well, I didn't meet them, but the fact that I had to pass their condo on the way to Dallas Rehab was too tempting, especially when I saw the van sitting in their driveway. Something went off inside me and I whipped my car off the freeway, turned around, and headed straight for their apartment.

After knocking twice, I heard movement inside and finally Clyde opened the door a crack. It was two p.m., but his bathrobe told me he had not even started getting ready to come see me. Well, they were seeing me now.

"I thought you were coming out to the house to talk." I could barely keep the fury out of my voice.

"I was."

I could tell he was cross because I had the audacity to show up at his door. Then I saw Judy. Her head was peering over Clyde's shoulder. I don't know how I got past this six-foot-three-inch, two hundred twenty-five pound man, but I went straight for her hair. I pulled her down right on top of me. I don't have a violent nature, but I started pulling her head up and down above me and screaming hysterically,

"Look what you've done to me! Look what you've done to me! You've turned me into a raving maniac! I'm not like this!"

Clyde tried to separate us, but he couldn't budge the hold I had on her. Judy couldn't get up and she couldn't get away. I don't know how long we stayed like that, but finally Clyde forced me to turn loose. He made me sit on the couch and said through clenched teeth,

"Now that you've pulled your little temper tantrum, are you ready to discuss this like an adult?"

I thought to myself, *How dare you both!* Suddenly, all I wanted was to get out of there.

They wanted me to stay and talk, but I couldn't stay in that place another minute.

"I don't want to discuss it anymore. I have nothing to say." I felt drained of energy and emotion. "I would have discussed this with you this morning, but now I have nothing to say. I see where I stand."

I got up and walked out. I slid wearily under the wheel of my car. When I looked in the visor mirror, I was a mess. My makeup was smeared, my hair a wreck, and one earring was missing.

Boy, I must have put on quite a show, I thought. *I've got to be insane. I've never done anything like that in my life.*

I stopped at a quick-stop to try to put myself back together. In the rest room mirror I could see blotches on my arms where Clyde had gripped me when he tried to get me away from Judy. Scratches were on my neck and face where Judy had left her own mark. This is what I had allowed myself to come to.

I HAD LOVED CLYDE ODOM SINCE I WAS THIRTEEN YEARS OLD AND HAD ALWAYS PICTURED US HAVING THE PERFECT MARRIAGE. BUT AFTER 23 YEARS, IT WAS NO LONGER PERFECT AND NO LONGER A MARRIAGE. (MY SENIOR HIGH SCHOOL PORTRAIT, WE'D ALREADY DATED SEVERAL YEARS)

ME, STACY AND TODD ON A PICNIC SEVERAL YEARS EARLIER.
YOU NEVER THINK YOU'RE GOING TO BE HAPPY AGAIN OR HAVE FUN AFTER
A TRAGEDY HAPPENS, BUT YOU CAN, AND YOU DO, AND YOU WILL.

CHAPTER 11
6 - 7 MONTHS — STARTING OVER

I didn't hear from or about them for quite awhile — only the little that Todd told me, and even Todd didn't see them much. We heard they had moved to a nicer place out in the country. Clyde had always liked the country, so I knew he was happy.

Clyde was so busy with his own life that he didn't have time for either of his children. He no longer even gave us money because he was angry at me. He was furious because I wouldn't agree to his demands in the divorce settlement. But resourcefulness was one of the things I had learned during the past year — my banker loaned me money for Todd, Stacy and me to live on for awhile.

In early November, with Thanksgiving fast approaching and Todd still in Dallas Rehab, Stacy and I began to have something of a life of our own. Each day she would go to school and I would go to Dallas Rehab. Leaving home about ten o'clock, I would drive into Dallas, stay with Todd until nine p.m., and get home around eleven. Stacy went in with me on Fridays and we would do something special with Todd, then bring him home with us on Saturday morning. And then we would take him back to Dallas Rehab by Sunday night. The days just seemed to fly by, and then before we knew it, Thanksgiving was upon us.

Unlike the 4th of July had been, the Thanksgiving Day holiday was a great time for us. Mark Mullins came over early and helped get Todd up. I am so grateful to Mark for all his help during that holiday weekend. His strength helped all of us have a really good time. The holiday went by much too fast — it was a truly wonderful Thanksgiving, and our lives, Todd's,

Stacy's and mine, seemed to be getting back on some kind of track. Then, early one morning, I got a call from Mamaw. She was frantic.

"Terry, Clyde's in the hospital and he's dying!"

"What hospital?" I felt distant from anything to do with Clyde anymore — but I loved Mamaw and she was very upset.

"Tyler," she answered. "He's got a blood clot or something in his head."

She wanted me to go to Tyler, a town in East Texas. That man had been living with another woman for three months and she wanted me to go to see about him? What right did she have to want me to go and see about him?

But I loved Mamaw as much as my own mother so I told her I would talk it over with Stacy. Stacy and I both felt she should go along. *Here we go again,* I thought.

I called Dallas Rehab to get a message to Todd that I wouldn't be there that day, deciding not to tell him anything about Clyde until I could find out what was wrong. Then I asked some friends at Dallas Rehab to look in on him but not to tell him about Clyde — Mamaw could have just been over-reacting.

When we got to the hospital, Clyde was in excruciating pain. He had been having headaches for several days and had taken nothing but aspirin, but that morning he began passing out. Judy, scared, took him to the hospital. The doctors said he had had an aneurysm, a bursting of a blood vessel leading to the brain, and he already had blood in his spinal column. They were offering no hope that he would pull through, but they planned to send him to Parkland Hospital in Dallas where he would have a better chance of survival. It was so serious they had already called in a specialist that would be standing by when he arrived.

I wanted to go in to see him. My feelings about Clyde were uncertain, but I was very sorry he was ill. I had gradually become separated from the commitment of being his wife, realizing I could have a life of my own apart from him, but nonetheless, I still, for some reason, wanted to see him. They said he might not even make the trip to Dallas, and this could be my last chance.

My in-laws wanted me to be at Parkland the next day when Clyde was brought to Parkland Hospital. So Mamaw, Stacy, Todd, Barbara, Jake, and I arrived at the hospital so early that morning we saw the ambulance as it pulled into the emergency parking area bringing Clyde from Tyler.

And right behind it pulled in Judy in the big fancy pickup truck she and Clyde had bought after both their vehicles had been confiscated. Judy got out of the truck and ran to catch up with the gurney. She had on high heels and was dressed to the "T". I watched as Clyde was wheeled in through the Emergency Room doors with Judy right behind him.

[Later on, I found out that just inside those double doors was a man waiting that I now believe God sent just for Clyde. I don't know all the particulars, but that man prayed the sinner's prayer with Clyde before he went up to ICU — and Clyde was still alert and able to respond.

I later met that same man when he came into the ICU waiting area and asked for Clyde's wife. I stepped up and said, "That is me."

He looked at me funny and said, "You're not the one I met downstairs!"

"Oh, you mean Judy," I said. "You can find her in the other waiting area." He left, but I didn't know the significance of his appearance until around Christmas Eve — I only tell it here because of its spiritual importance to me.]

After we watched Clyde being taken into the Emergency Room, Mamaw, Stacy, Todd, Barbara, Jake, and I went in and were directed to the intensive care waiting room. We sat quietly waiting for news. Todd had insisted on coming with Stacy and me after I told him about his dad. In the waiting room he struck up a conversation with a young boy about his age. Todd introduced Stacy and me to the boy and his mom.

Then Judy walked into the room and the boy pointed at her.

"See, Mom," he said. "I told you that's Todd's mom."

Judy saw us and immediately became very huffy. It seems she had been telling everyone that her name was Judy Odom, that she was Clyde's wife and Todd's mother. Why she would do this, I did not know, but I could surmise and suddenly, I became very impatient and angry with her. Clyde was still my husband — I was the mother of his children, and I had the legal right and responsibility to make decisions about Clyde's care — especially since I held the insurance and documentation that would take care of all of his hospital expenses!

Judy was very upset, but I found it hard to pity her, after all — she had moved in on my family. However, when I got the chance, I tried to be generous with my former friend and told her I was not trying to destroy what she and Clyde had or could potentially have.

Far be it for Clyde's wife to come between him and the one he loves! I thought sarcastically.

"I simply have a responsibility as his wife and the mother of his children to be here, and like it or not, I intend to be here," I told her.

I had been legally advised that since our insurance and property were involved, I needed to assert my role as Clyde's legal wife in case he didn't survive. To Judy, that may have sounded cold since she had been living with Clyde for several months, but I had a son that would need care for the rest of his life. I couldn't afford to make a mistake that would affect all of us in the future just because Judy wanted to pretend to be Clyde's wife, and because of my own pride and rejection.

But, to keep peace in the waiting room, I agreed to let Judy go in to see Clyde during the first visiting time. We (his family) would go in later.

The first time I saw Clyde, he had an airway in his mouth that went down into his lungs to help him breathe and he couldn't speak. As I watched him lying there so helpless, I thought, *How strange — all of this with Todd, and now Clyde, has happened within six months.*

Looking down at Clyde, I realized there was still love in my heart for my husband, but I knew he would always hurt me. He would never be faithful. I could tell Clyde was glad I was there by the way he looked at me and squeezed my hand. I was crying as I bent down and whispered,

"Please don't ever get to where we can't talk to one another again. I know you've chosen Judy, but there are things in our lives we need to share, like the kids."

I was ready to accept the fact that our marriage was really over, but for Todd's and Stacy's sake, we needed to be friends.

The doctors gave Clyde a one percent chance to live if they operated and no chance if they didn't. We had no choice — surgery was scheduled for the next morning. So there we were again, only this time, it was the daddy. We met in one of the ICU waiting rooms, except for Judy. She was quite indignant that I was there at all, so she chose to wait in a waiting room down the hall. So, Mamaw, Clyde's sister Barbara and her husband Jake, Todd, Stacy and I waited those long hours together.

After surgery, Clyde was paralyzed on his left side. He knew us, but he seemed like a different man. During the days that followed, our lives became even more of a nightmare. Christmas was approaching, but none of us were looking forward to it.

Todd wanted to be with his dad, he and Stacy loved Clyde very much. And, since Todd insisted on being with his dad everyday. I would drop Mamaw off at Parkland Hospital, then Stacy and I would drive to Dallas Rehab, pick up Todd and then drive back to the hospital. (Todd was missing therapy sessions so he could see his dad.)

I had spent so much of the last six months in waiting rooms, I had become numb. Clyde was in intensive care and we could only see him for a few moments at very specific times: twelve, three, six and eight p.m. The hospital was very strict in permitting visitors to only come during those specified times. This was very trying for all of us and I kept hoping our lives would somehow get back to normal, or anywhere close to it.

The visiting situation was, to say the least, very unusual. Judy took her turn to see Clyde, then me and the kids would take our turn. Seeing the woman who had contributed to the breakup of my marriage was very stressful. I didn't understand why I would still put myself through this! It became so difficult to face Judy every visiting time that I finally thought the solution would be to let her have her own specific time to see Clyde — the kids, Mamaw and I would take the others. I asked her if she'd mind taking the first two visits and give us the two evening visits. Judy agreed that it would be a much better arrangement for everyone. It was also better for

Todd because he wouldn't miss his therapy sessions. Throughout this whole ordeal, the Lord continued to be my strength and He kept me going.

Clyde had a tube about one inch in diameter in his mouth that went into his lungs so he could breathe, just like Todd had in the beginning. Also, because he couldn't speak, he had to communicate with his eyes — just as Todd had done. I think that this is when he began to lean on me more than Judy because I could understand him by watching the expression in his eyes — we had been married over 23 years and knew each other so very well. Clyde also knew I would be there if he needed me and I don't think he was so sure that Judy would. After he had recovered a bit, we could also communicate because he had slowly begun to write with his "good" hand. He would begin a sentence and I would know before the sentence was completed what he wanted.

He would write notes such as "I need wa—," or "Wet my l—," but he wouldn't even have to complete the sentence and would just draw a line to the end of the page because I was already performing what he needed. I knew immediately that he needed a drink of water or he wanted me to wet a washcloth and wet his lips. Whatever Clyde needed, he would have to write it. It was very difficult to make out exactly what he was writing, but I had learned to communicate with Todd, so it made it easier for me to understand Clyde. I'd also known Clyde since I was 13 years old, and knew him like I knew no other person — on the other hand, Judy would get very frustrated because she couldn't understand him.

Then one day I came in alone to see Clyde. He pointed to the paper on the night stand letting me know he wanted to write something. As he slowly began to scribble his message to me, I watched in amazement as he wrote "I love y—," and then pointed to me.

What is going on? I thought to myself.

I felt very confused. I was just getting used to living without Clyde and I didn't know if I could handle being drawn back into his life. Mentally, I had really taken a back seat to Judy who had begun to assume the public role of Clyde's "wife," and I had also heard through one of Judy's visitors that she and Clyde had started going to church before his aneurysm. (Of course, I remembered the charges were still pending from their arrest and wondered if this was a sincere attempt to repent or just a cover up to make them look good to the authorities.)

Oh, whatever! I just wanted to do what was right. "Lord, are you bringing Clyde and I back together?" I wondered out loud.

I decided I would make an appointment with the pastor of the church that Clyde and Judy had been attending. I wanted to know how he felt about their relationship. If he indicated that they were destined to be together, then I would know what to do.

I called the minister and he very graciously agreed to see me. Mamaw agreed to go with me for the appointment. We made our way to his lovely home across town from the hospital. It was late when we arrived. (After meeting him, I remembered that we had previously met when he came to visit Clyde at the hospital.)

We talked for a long time and I poured my heart out to him, telling him about Clyde's unfaithfulness to me over the years of our marriage, but also telling him that I still loved Clyde and I knew he still loved me. The minister's advice to me was very scriptural: If there's a chance for a marriage to work, then the right thing to do is to make it work. We prayed over the whole situation and I left feeling very confused. Later in the car, I looked over at my mother-in-law.

"I can't believe God wants Clyde and me back together."

But it sure looked that way, and I was determined to be quiet and let the Holy Spirit lead me. Things were happening too fast in my life — frightening things. I didn't know if I was coming or going. I knew that scripturally, it was OK for me to divorce because of infidelity — and Clyde had been committing adultery throughout our marriage — but I also knew that God could take even the worst marriage and turn it around.

Christmas was upon us and I just couldn't work up any joy for the season. It had been seven months since Todd's accident, and the doctors still were not ready to release him. Now Clyde was paralyzed, barely able to communicate, and our divorce had been filed. Looking forward to that Christmas season, I was definitely *not* filled with joy.

TODD...

FROM ONE CHRISTMAS TO THE NEXT

But there was one thing that we were thankful for — a lady we did not even know insisted we stay in her condominium near the hospital while she was out of town. It was already decorated for Christmas, and helped tremendously to brighten our spirits.

For the kid's sake I tried to muster up some Christmas spirit. We decided to do a little Christmas shopping — but while we were shopping Mamaw was snooping.

"Terry," she confided. "I've been watching those two, and it's very interesting. When Judy goes in to visit Clyde, he keeps his eyes closed and doesn't pay any attention to her, but when you and the kids go in, he's alert and glad to see you."

I knew, by the notes he wrote, Clyde was ready to come home. He wanted to be with me and his kids. Poor Judy. She didn't know what was going on, and I didn't feel I should tell her. Clyde loved me and I could finally admit that I still loved him — but he had gotten himself into this mess and he could get himself out of it. I maintained neutral ground, staying away from Judy as much as possible. With our divided visiting times — Judy visiting Clyde in the morning, me and the kids and our family in the evening — it was just easier for everybody.

Knowing that Clyde was still in love with me and wanted our family back together again, that Christmas Eve night became a joyous time for us. I picked Todd up from Dallas Rehab, and he and I spent time with Clyde and Mamaw. We gave Clyde a wristwatch we had bought him. Stacy was at her aunt's house spending Christmas Eve with the family and they planned to go to my mother's later. I felt so good, like everything was right again. I knew it was just a matter of time until we would be together again — a real family. I longed for a normal family relationship — this time with spiritual ties.

Clyde had prayed the prayer of salvation with a man when he had first come into the hospital — the man just inside the Emergency Room doors. I felt it was probably because he was scared, but I hoped it meant more than that. Christmas Eve night, that same man who had prayed with Clyde came to see him and told us how he had been into drugs and how God had set him free.

"You can be set free, too," he told Clyde.

I could not believe how God orchestrated to send someone who, just like Clyde, had been involved in drugs. What a mighty God we serve! This man gave up his time with his family to come to witness to us at the hospital. I don't know his name, nor where he lives, but I'll never forget him. I had prayed for Clyde to be saved since I was fifteen years old. I wanted so much for him to be a Christian husband and father, and if it took Todd's accident and Clyde's aneurysm to bring it about and to make us a real family, I felt it was worth it.

I'll never forget as Christmas Eve rolled into Christmas day. I was so grateful for the loan of that wonderful condo so Stacy, Mamaw and I could stay close to the hospital. Early that morning, we just couldn't wait for the late visiting time to see Clyde. So before Judy arrived, Stacy and I sneaked a quick visit with him. Then we watched out a window from the fifth floor as Judy arrived.

Judy pulled into the parking lot in my husband's brand new truck. She was a knockout in one of the designer outfits she loved to wear — long off-white cape, matching high heeled boots and all the right accessories. Stacy and I continued to watch her as, with wrapped gift in hand, she crossed by the crosswalk and disappeared into the hospital. She was so beautiful. I thought of all the years that Judy had been hooked on drugs — she didn't have a clue as to what life was all about — but nothing had affected her physical beauty. It was only later that I found out that Judy's gift to Clyde had been a wedding band. She still assumed everything between the two of them was fine, they'd marry and live happily ever after. She didn't know that Clyde's feelings had changed.

New Year's Eve came and we planned to spend the day with Clyde. I knew that we wouldn't have to worry about Judy because she would never miss an opportunity to party. Mamaw, Todd, Stacy and I had a good time with Clyde — we were even allowed to stay a little longer because of the holiday.

After the first of the year, Clyde's doctors started talking about taking him out of intensive care and putting him into a room. He was still on the ventilator, but during the past month his doctor had removed the tube from his mouth and inserted a trache into his windpipe.

After the tube was removed from his mouth, I noticed Clyde would try to speak although he couldn't make a sound because of the trache. His mouth and tongue moved in a different kind of way, sort of crooked. I thought, *Oh, well. We'll deal with that when the time comes.* Until then, it was time to move on.

In the past few days, Clyde had started writing in his notes that when it was time for him to be moved to a room, he wanted me to stay with him. (The hospital could accommodate me in another bed in his room.)

"But, what about Judy?" I asked.

"You!" was all he would write.

The doctors and nurses were very sympathetic to me as they watched our little soap opera unfold.

Moving day finally came. It was time for Clyde to leave intensive care. I knew that he'd had time to think about everything and that once again he wanted his family together as much as I did. The hospital called me at my mother's to tell me that they were moving him around ten o'clock and they felt that I should know. It was very difficult for me. *What about Judy?* I kept wondering.

I wanted Clyde to tell Judy — not me! It was his place to end his affair, not mine. I was also trying to be sensitive to the fact that Judy didn't even know that Clyde no longer cared for her. (In my efforts to not be nasty and hurtful, I think that I was somewhat overly sensitive to her feelings, but I think that the non-Christian part of me really couldn't have cared less.)

Stacy and I immediately headed back to the hospital to face this next challenge. Since Judy didn't even know that Clyde was to be moved that day, we came in through the back of the hospital so we wouldn't run into her. However, even with all the extra precautions, she saw us. We hurried up to ICU. The nurse let us in shutting the door in Judy's face, leaving her standing there very confused. (The nurses had always treated us well, I could see what they thought about Judy.)

"Clyde, they're going to move you to a room today," I told him. He was still very sick, so he was pretty much out of it. I needed to know if he wanted me to actually be with him, if he was really coming back to us, or if I should step aside for Judy — Judy and I both deserved to know that.

"Clyde, listen to me," my hand on his arm was gentle but firm as I tried to rouse him from his groggy sleep.

"The time is here — what do you want to do, Clyde?" I asked urgently. "Do you want me to go with you up to your room and stay with you, or do you want Judy? Just tell me. Whatever you choose, I'll understand."

Clyde pointed toward me as if to say he chose me.

"Fine," I said. "But you'll have to tell Judy."

Judy was still standing just outside the ICU door, wondering what was going on. Clyde wrote me a note telling me to tell her.

"No," I said emphatically. "It's not my responsibility to tell her."

He gave me a pitiful look as if to say, *But I'm sick*.

"You're the one who is making this decision," I said to him. "And you're going to tell her. It's not right for it to come from me."

I walked outside so the attendants could get him ready to move to his room. Judy sensed something was going on, but she didn't know what.

"What are you doing here, Terry?"

"Clyde wants me to stay with him and take care of him."

I had not intended to say that, it just popped out — it would have been so much better coming from Clyde. Judy's mouth dropped open.

"He'll have to tell me that," she said, haughtily.

"That's between you two," I said.

Judy whirled around and went into his room. Clyde got very frustrated as he tried to tell her what he wanted, but she seemed to understand. Her face was a mixture of hurt and stiff upper lip pride when she rejoined me outside intensive care. I tried to be reasonable.

"Judy," I said. "I'm not trying to take anything from you that's not already mine. I don't know how this is going to turn out, I just know that at this time he feels more comfortable with me taking care of him."

I knew it was probably the fact that we had been together for so many years, but I was willing to take the chance.

"If you and Clyde are meant to be together, it will happen. And later, if you want to be with him and he wants to be with you, that's okay, too. If you want to see him when he gets in his room, then I'll leave so you can spend some time with him."

"Okay," she agreed meekly. "I'd like to come back this evening."

"Fine," I was relieved that she seemed to accept the arrangement.

I left her alone with Clyde when she came to see him in his room that evening. But, when I saw her leave later, I knew by the stricken look on her face it was over between her and Clyde. I knew she wouldn't be back. Whether it was because Clyde needed us since he was so ill or because he really wanted us, my family was back together. I would not let myself speculate on why this happened — I was just enjoying having my husband back. I wondered if Judy would have really taken care of him if he had chosen her. I just couldn't picture her in that role. Of course it was up to me now, and I knew it wouldn't be easy.

ME, MAMAW, CLYDE, STACY AND TODD
EASTER 1986 – WE'RE ALL DOING GREAT...

CHAPTER 12
8 MONTHS — TWO INVALIDS

The days passed in a blur. There was a roll away cot in Clyde's room and I stayed there at night — then I'd go to Dallas Rehab, pick up Todd and bring him to the hospital to stay with his dad during the day. It was already mid-January.

Physically, Todd was much better. He was regaining a little movement in his left arm. The doctors at Dallas Rehab were hopeful that he would be able to come home in an electric wheelchair which he could maneuver himself. That would help tremendously.

Things were looking up and I felt a joy inside I had never felt. I was tired but I was happy. The joy I felt now was because of my walk with the Lord. I had trusted Him to work things out for us and He had. *Who knows,* I thought, *Todd could even regain more use of his body.* I knew nothing was impossible with God.

Clyde began the weaning process from the ventilator. He was improving physically, but his personality had gone through a change since he'd been sick. He was like a different person, irritable and hateful and so very angry. Todd had gone through the same process — so I knew not being able to breathe on his own was very trying for Clyde.

Day by day, the staff plugged off a little more of the trache allowing more air to be rerouted to his own airway. Clyde felt he was not getting enough oxygen and it was very difficult for him. Clyde and I had become really close since he had been in the hospital. Watching my once strong husband go through this illness was very difficult for me. Dealing with Clyde's change in personality and temperament was even more challenging.

I wondered what I had done to deserve this. Here I was, doing my best, trying to take care of my husband and my son, and never seeming to have time for Stacy or myself. It would have been so easy to allow self-pity to take control, but I could not let that happen. Who else would do what I was doing? It was my responsibility and besides, I wanted to be the one to take care of both of them. It was enough that my family was together — that was all that mattered.

It was exciting when they finally were able to remove the trache from Clyde's throat. I was anxious to hear his voice again. It wasn't that easy — when he tried to speak, the sound was unintelligible. One side of his vocal cord was still paralyzed. He not only could not talk, he couldn't swallow. I had to learn to feed him through a feeding tube that was inserted into his stomach. *Maybe I should become a full fledged nurse,* I thought. *During the last few months I certainly have been getting the training.*

Clyde was glad I was there to take care of him, but his temper was always ready to flare. He had always been a calm person, but now he flew off the handle at the least little thing. Even when he was being unfaithful he had never been unkind to me — so I found it hard to handle this new Clyde and his temper. When I couldn't cope with him, I'd announce, "Hey, I'm getting out of here," and I would just walk off and leave him.

Clyde couldn't believe I'd just walk out on him. He didn't realize how strong I'd had to become to take care of Todd. I had discovered I could take just so much, then I had to walk away to keep from losing myself. After I worked out my feelings, I would go back. Todd was always ready to forgive — Clyde was having to learn to cope with the new me, too.

A real dilemma presented itself when the time came for Todd to be released from Dallas Rehab. Clyde had a few more weeks in the hospital, but I knew Todd would need around-the-clock care. Clyde and I discussed it. (I could understand his speech a little better now, though it was still far from perfect.)

"Terry, I know Todd needs you. Go on home with him if you want to," he said.

But, it was clear he really wanted me to stay with him when he suggested his mother could go home with the kids. We finally reached the decision to hire a private nurse to help Clyde's mother and I would stay with Clyde. I knew Todd was anxious to go home. It had been eight long months since he had lived at home. I felt he would cooperate and everything would be all right.

MY LOVE FOR CLYDE HAD ENDURED SINCE 1962
AND I WASN'T READY TO GIVE IT UP

TODD... MY SON

GETTING A MOMENT TO MYSELF ON OUR PATIO

CHAPTER 13
9 MONTHS — HOME

Then came the big day when Todd was to leave Dallas Rehabilitation Institute. We met with the staff and our family to discuss how it would be done. Clyde and his mother agreed that since I needed to stay with him while he was in the hospital, she would stay with Todd and Stacy until both Clyde and I could come home. All of the details were worked out and then we discussed Todd's future.

Although Todd still tired easily, I thought it would be good for him to start back to school at midterm — at least for half a day. With his accident happening Memorial weekend at the end of his freshman year, Todd had only missed one semester of school, but he had been away from our home and his friends for eight months. Mentally, he was fine and I felt his life should be as normal as possible — and that included going back to school.

I knew if Todd sat at home he'd brood over his condition. I had to fight everyone — no one agreed with me except Stacy. But having him in school right away was very important to me, it would bring some normalcy to his life. And I desperately wanted my son to start to feel that his life could be normal again.

Todd's nurse, a nurse's aide, Stacy, Clyde's mother, his sister and her husband gathered to bring Todd home. Thankfully, the trip to our home was uneventful.

At home, things worked pretty well with everyone helping. Mamaw would get Todd up in the morning and manage to get him bathed and dressed — but she said she would not get him up to go to school because she thought it was too soon.

"Mamaw, I'm taking care of your son, and I expect you to take care of mine," I told her.

"I won't get him up to go to school," she repeated defiantly.

"Okay, then I'll come home and do it myself," I told her.

Clyde thought I was being foolish. But I was determined to give Todd this chance to get on with his life.

"I'm going home," I said. "Todd needs me and he needs to go to school with his friends. You'll just have to stay by yourself."

Clyde finally agreed. I don't know if it was because he decided I was right or if he just knew I'd do it anyway. But I knew this was right for Todd. He would be going only half a day, but at least he'd be in touch with the normal world again.

It felt so good being home, sleeping in my own bed and eating breakfast in my own kitchen. I got Todd up for his first day of school and got him dressed. I took extra care because I wanted him to look special his first day back. We were both a little nervous but Todd looked great and I felt terrific. I was so proud of him.

"Okay," Mamaw said. "I'm sorry, Terry. You go back and spend the rest of the time with Clyde. We'll take care of things here." She smiled sheepishly. "We'll get Todd off to school."

I had won this battle and it felt good, but as I lay on the bed in Clyde's hospital room that night, I was very troubled.

Lord, I thought. *What is ahead for me, what have I got myself into? Starting a marriage over with a husband who is partially paralyzed and a son who is totally paralyzed. Todd needs so much care, he can't even turn over in bed by himself. Lord,* I prayed silently. *Todd can't scratch his nose or comb his hair. He won't ever be able to bathe himself. Lord, you're going to have to stay real close to me, because I've got a tough trip ahead of me.* I fell into a restless sleep, feeling the heaviness of the future.

The next morning I awoke feeling happy and glad to be alive. I felt a new courage inside, not for the future I was still unsure of, but for my life that I resolved to deal with one step at a time. I began to concentrate on helping Clyde get better, so we could go home and be a family again.

The doctors were amazed at Clyde's progress, and knowing our situation at home, decided to release him early. Since I had been trained to take care of Todd and his personal needs, they felt sure I would be able to take care of Clyde with his breathing apparatus and feeding tube. Now I would be taking both Clyde and Todd for therapy at Dallas Rehab.

It was February, nine long months since Todd's accident and I was really excited the day I packed up Clyde's stuff and we set off toward Emory in the van that would now not only accommodate Todd's wheelchair, but Clyde's, too. Somehow we would make it. If I could handle Todd, I could handle Clyde. I was exultant. Our homecoming was very special for me. My family was together again — struggling maybe — but we were together.

Todd was getting on with his life. Five days a week I got him up, dressed and off to a half day of school. Todd hated going to school now — it was a challenge just to get him to go. At the end of his freshman year he had looked forward to being on the varsity football team. Now, everything had changed for him.

Sometimes he only stayed one period, but at least he was out there. I was convinced more than ever that getting out and going to school was good for him. Teachers were patient with him and the kids were glad to have him back.

Clyde was still recuperating and had to stay in bed. He was getting better and stronger every day and seemed truly glad to be home with us.

Our home soon became a very active, busy household, with not only the cooking, cleaning, laundry, and just daily living, but the house itself was getting a major overhaul. Men were knocking down walls, building ramps and every other conceivable thing that would make it accessible for wheelchairs.

Todd was determined to go where he wanted and he wasn't going to let anything get in his way. We were all so happy to be home.

Spring was especially beautiful that year, bursting with the stark white of the dogwoods and the colorful redbuds and yellow daffodils. *This is what Heaven will look like,* I thought. It was so good to work outside, mowing the grass and tending the neglected flower beds.

I wanted Todd to be able to get out into the woods, to sit and hear the birds singing and watch the squirrels running from tree to tree. I mowed the grass in a spot that actually went into the woods around our house so that Todd could take his chair down there and actually feel and hear nature around him.

Life was good — my husband was back, Todd was back, and Stacy was glad to have her family back, too. We had so much time to make up with her. She had been such a trooper through all the rough times, never making demands, just standing back, ready to do whatever was needed. Stacy had had to miss so much of her own teenage time, but maybe now things could really be normal for her, or as normal as it could be with both her brother and dad in wheelchairs, and a mom who was still occupied more as a nurse than a mother.

I was also looking forward to the time when I could concentrate a little more on being a wife to Clyde. We had become friends, able to talk and share with each other, but I missed the closeness of the physical love my husband and I had shared for so many years. I felt he had really changed and wanted to be a husband to me, even encouraging me to make plans for us to go to a marriage enrichment seminar at a little church in East Texas. We spent a whole day there. We had never experienced anything like it — it was wonderful. Clyde really seemed to want things to be right between us.

My family started attending a little church in Emory, Texas. Stacy and Todd had gone there a few times before Todd's accident. Everyone was very friendly and warm. It felt good to be in church again.

I noticed Clyde was responding to the messages preached by Brother Walker, a big rough talking minister. When Clyde and I had been young teenagers, I had attended a revival and requested prayer for him to give his life to God. The ministers that I talked to said they would visit Clyde. I worried what Clyde would do when they talked with him and prayed that he would listen and be "saved". Clyde hadn't listened. Now he was forty-three years old and he'd never made any kind of a commitment to God. After all these years, here was a minister Clyde would listen to.

One afternoon Stacy and I were coming in from shopping, and Todd came rolling his chair out to meet us with his big heart-melting grin. We knew something special was up.

"Mama, Todd said. "I've got a big surprise for you. Hurry and come on inside. Daddy has something he wants to tell you."

I was almost afraid to go in. I knew Brother Walker had come over that day to see Clyde and hope rose in me.

"What do you want to tell me, Clyde?" Thankful tears were already clouding my vision.

Clyde looked up at me from his recliner. With a big grin on his face, he announced,

"I've been saved."

"Praise the Lord!" I shouted, swiping at my tears with a trembling hand. "I've been praying for this for so many years."

I had dreamed of having a spiritual relationship with my husband, but had long ago concluded it would never happen. It was the sweetest time of our married life. This time, Clyde's conversion was real — not something he had done out of fear, or that he was talked into. He was very open and excited and wanted to talk about his commitment to Jesus.

That Sunday, I sensed a new excitement in my family as we dressed for church. There was no last minute dawdling, no arguing. As we got out of the van at the church, I made sure everyone's clothes were straight and their hair was in place. Todd dodged my hand good-naturedly and I gave him a playful swat on the side of his head, then we made our way into the church along with friends who had slowed down to walk with us.

I don't remember the sermon that day, but I'll never forget the pastor's altar call. When the invitation was given for those who wanted to confess Jesus as their Savior to come forward, I saw Clyde step into the aisle and start toward the altar. He was using a walker now and I let him go by himself. This was something I couldn't help him do. He needed to take this walk on his own.

But, after he had talked to the pastor a few minutes, I walked down the aisle myself. With all the things that were going on in my life, it would be a good time to rededicate my own life to the Lord.

I had just taken my place beside Clyde when I heard the familiar creak of Todd's chair — Todd and Stacy had joined us. The four of us repeated our promise to live for God and to trust Him for whatever lay ahead. Clyde made arrangements to be baptized in a couple of weeks — and since I wanted us both to have a new beginning, I asked to be baptized along with him.

"I never — in my whole life — expected to feel like this," I told Clyde as we were driving home that night. "I feel like you and I are as clean and pure as the driven snow. We have a new life ahead of us."

In the dim light I saw Clyde agree with a solemn nod.

LAVERNE MORRIS AND HER SONS MARK AND "LITTLE TODD" WHO HELPED BE TODD'S LEGS AND ARMS FOR THAT FIRST YEAR. LAVERNE HELPED TODD FINISH UP HIS HIGH SCHOOL REQUIREMENTS SO THAT HE COULD GRADUATE WITH HIS FRIENDS. MARK BECAME ONE OF TODD'S BEST FRIENDS.

CHAPTER 14
WHEN DREAMS DIE

The following week a redhead named Laverne Morris came into my life. She wheeled into our driveway bringing a banana cream pie — and a friendship that would last for years. I didn't realize how starved I was for female companionship, someone to just talk with and share girl talk.

Laverne attended the same church in Emory our family had just joined. She had met Todd and Stacy when they were attending by themselves — before Todd's accident.

"My son, Mark, is a big boy," she said. "But when I saw Todd in the choir standing in front of my son, Todd almost dwarfed him."

Laverne said when she heard about Todd's accident she immediately felt a bonding with my family. Laverne had such a bubbly personality that she made me feel alive when I was with her.

As we talked, we made a startling discovery. Her father, a minister, pastored the church my family attended when I was a child. And now here she was in my kitchen, drinking coffee and putting the finishing touches on the most perfect time of my life. *[What a small world it is — I had been best friends in Dallas with Laverne's cousin Ginger through both grade school, then Junior High. Laverne was about five years younger than Ginger and me, so I never really paid attention to her at that time since she was so much younger.]*

Laverne brought more than a banana cream pie that day, she brought a lifeline, and she became my very dearest friend.

Life had taken on a new meaning for me, with what seemed like a brand new family. But things were still hectic, and my routine was still tough.

Todd...

Every morning, getting Todd up, bathed and dressed took an hour and a half. Lifting this two hundred sixty pound son of mine was quite an ordeal. First, we used his old chair so I could roll him into the kitchen to shampoo his hair in the sink. I used the lift on the back of his chair to get him in position. Then I would set him back up and roll him into the game room, to his electric chair, and then do a manual lift from one chair to the other.

I was still determined he was going to look his very best when he faced the world every day. I knew he needed to have this at least, to help him feel good about himself, to help him have the self confidence he needed.

Things had settled down to a workable routine, and everything was going great — or so I thought.

But Clyde had been getting restless. Life just wasn't exciting for him since he couldn't do the things he wanted.

"I don't understand why I'm not well yet," he'd grumble. "I made this commitment to God, it looks like he could heal me. And what about Todd? Why doesn't God get him out of that chair?"

He began questioning whether he was even saved. He didn't seem as happy to be home as he did at first, and he started being hateful to me.

I tried to help him and to be understanding, but I knew that one of things that was worrying Clyde was that no one in our family was working. He felt responsible for all of us. I understood — Clyde wasn't able to work and it would be hard for me to work and take care of both Todd and Clyde.

We discussed the possibility of my going to our liquor store and taking charge of the business — then the money would be ours instead of paying it out to employees. Finally, we decided that I should go over to the store and start reorganizing.

Nita, who Clyde had hired before his accident, was managing the store. I had always suspected that she was more than just an employee, but hadn't really thought about her since Todd's accident and then Clyde's poor health had occupied my thoughts and life. After Todd's accident and Clyde had left me for Judy, I'd forgotten about Nita.

Clyde's health kept improving and he began to use a cane instead of the walker. He was still partially paralyzed and talked with an unnatural nasal sound, but he could communicate and get around pretty well.

As his health improved, Clyde began coming over to the store while I was there. At the store, he seemed to be a little happier, a little more like himself — but when we were home, he'd be hateful to me and mean.

I didn't understand what was going wrong. Mamaw, who was staying with us most of the time, noticed and commented on his behavior.

Finally, I realized that Clyde's face lit up only when Nita our store manager was around. With her, he was happy.

I had lived with Clyde too long not to recognize the signs. *Surely, he wouldn't be fooling around in his condition,* I thought. *Didn't this man ever quit?*

Clyde's health continued to improve and he took over working at the store. After he and Nita started closing the store, he'd come home at least an hour later than normal.

Full of dread and not wanting to believe it possible that he was yet again involved with someone else, I put two and two together — it was too much. I couldn't go through this again — not with everything else that had happened. Everything that I had been through in the past year with Todd and then Clyde had made me strong. A determination arose within me.

Before his illness, Clyde had always been very easy going. Even so, I had never talked back to him. It wasn't my way. After his aneurism and his personality changed, Clyde found it very hard to accept that I no longer gave in to him (such as I had done before in selling my first Merle Norman store, and then later on, the other one). Clyde was becoming more and more violent. One night he'd even held a lit cigarette to my cheek to make me do something he wanted. Another time, he'd tried to strangle me and left bruises on my throat.

Well, this is one affair that Clyde's not getting away with, I told myself. *If he has truly betrayed us yet again, it's over.* I had felt that the Holy Spirit was keeping me in our marriage so that it could be healed, and that could have happened. But, I also understood, finally, that I had really tried everything I could to hold our marriage together and I would feel no guilt or shame in letting the marriage go. Clyde and I were definitely "unequally yoked."

But, I couldn't confront Clyde and end the relationship unless I had proof. I needed to see with my own eyes. Always before when I had suspected that Clyde was seeing someone, I would always try and catch him, and, after a confrontation, he would always come back to me. This time would be different.

I thought that if I could just catch Clyde in the act — where there could be no denial on his part, or hiding my head in the sand on my part — that I would finally be able to let go and move on with my life. This time it would be very different.

I started going over to the store and watching from the outside while Clyde and Nita closed up. The liquor store was located in a shopping center that was on our property. There was a chain link fence between a motel and the store. I'd park the car behind the fence and watch the door until they came out.

One night after the lights went off, they didn't come out. Stacy (who had wanted to come with me at the last moment) and I waited and waited, but Clyde and Nita were still inside the store.

"I'm going over there and see if I can hear anything," I told Stacy as I opened the door.

"Mama, don't!" Stacy hissed, grabbing my arm. "Daddy'll hurt you!"

With my heart pounding, and feeling a little ashamed of myself, I went around to the back, but I couldn't hear anything. *I've got keys to the store,* I thought remembering Clyde's keys were in his truck which we were driving that night. I ran quickly back to the truck where Stacy was waiting nervously, and pulled the keys from the ignition.

"What are you doing, Mama? Let's get out of here before something bad happens."

Unable to stop myself, I made my way in the dim light to the back of the store and quietly let myself into the storeroom. Careful not to bump into anything, I crept to the front of the store, my vision limited to the security lights, but no one was there. I eased around to the office door, and I could hear them inside. I tried to peep through the glass, but I couldn't see anything.

I reached to open the door, and they saw me.

Dang it! I fumed. *He's put up two-way mirrors.*

"Oh, no! It's Terry!" I heard Nita say.

I could hear them frantically scrambling around inside, jeans being pulled on hastily, belt buckles clanking.

Anger boiled up inside of me and I started senselessly throwing bottles through the glass door. The shattered pieces flew everywhere. *How could he?* I screamed inside, sick and totally out of control.

Clyde, now fully clothed, jerked the office door open. He was furious. I ran from the store. What made me think it would be different this time? Did I really think Clyde had changed, or did I want my family together so much I just buried my head in the sand. How could I be so stupid?

Clyde came out of the store right behind me, so mad that, if he could have caught me, I really believe that he would have tried to hurt me. After all, he'd tried before.

I hurried to the pickup and jumped in locking the door as I blindly pushed the key into the ignition. The little car bounced over the mounds of dirt that had been left by construction workers as we tore off toward home.

"Mama!" Stacy cried. "What happened?"

I didn't want to tell Stacy what her Dad was doing, and as I drove frantically away from the store, I wasn't so sure what really did happen. Was I just imagining things? Did what I heard mean what I had assumed it did?

"Come on, Terry," I mumbled to myself. "Look at his record."

I screeched into the driveway not taking the time to park correctly. Leaving the keys dangling, I grabbed Stacy's hand and we ran through the garage and the back door. I headed immediately for Todd's room, where I knew I would find Todd and Mamaw, and I would be safe. Clyde would never do anything to me in front of Todd or his mother.

"What's wrong?" they both asked as I ran in out of breath.

"When Clyde comes home, he's going to kill me!" I blurted.

Leaping into bed with Todd, I quickly pulled the covers over me. Todd and Mamaw stared at me in astonishment.

Then we heard the sound — the deliberate, measured steps forced by paralysis and assisted by a cane. *Slide... Clump... Tap... Slide... Clump... Tap...* Clyde was coming toward us.

Suddenly the door burst open and Clyde stood, fists clenched, with fire flashing from his eyes. When he saw his mother and Todd his anger was immediately masked to avoid letting them see the rage he always tried to hide from everyone but me. He stood for a few moments in the doorway, then wordlessly turned and walked away. I stayed in Todd's bed the rest of the night, not wanting to face Clyde's anger. I felt safe, and Todd, even though he could only move his head, felt every bit the protector.

The next morning Clyde had calmed down some, but I was ready to explode. Gritting my teeth to keep myself under control, I confronted Clyde. There would be no mistake that I meant what I was saying.

"No more," I said. "This is the end for me. I'll take care of you like I take care of Todd. I'll be your nurse, but I won't sleep in your bed. I can't run away this time — I have no where to go but here. I know it's my responsibility, but I will not live with you as your wife. Do you understand me?" I calmed down, but with a finality long in coming, I added, "As far as I'm concerned, it's over."

The next day Clyde packed his clothes and left us once again — this time I knew it was for good. Even if he wanted to come back, this time I wouldn't let him.

Clyde's health had continued to improve and he was able to walk pretty well with his cane. I wonder what would have happened if he had been faithful to us and kept his commitment to God. We'll never know. I do know he was soon back on his walker, but he definitely did me a favor the day he walked out. I had all I could handle just taking care of Todd.

I don't know what I would have done during those days if it had not been for Laverne. The day she came into our lives with the banana cream pie, began a friendship that was to carry me through many rough days. She was my sounding board, someone I could go to when I needed to cry, or when I just needed to talk. Laverne was divorced, and she and her two boys spent many nights at our house. The bond between our two families grew stronger each day.

CHAPTER 15
15 MONTHS — MOVIN' ON

Summer came to an end and soon school would be starting — Stacy would be a sophomore at Emory and Todd would be going back to school full time as a junior. His sophomore year had been a real struggle and he'd had to take correspondence courses during the summer to catch up with his class so that he would graduate with them. Todd really didn't want to go to school, but I was determined that he finish — he needed to.

Mark, Laverne's oldest, was Todd's age and they were good friends. But it was Laverne's youngest son, also named Todd, who became Todd's buddy. To eliminate confusion, we called him "Little Todd". "Little Todd was Todd's constant companion in those beginning months and days before Todd out grew him, and his classmates in his Junior began to befriend him as buddies again. Little Todd was a gift from God for Todd.

Clyde had moved to the farm we owned, and was living in a mobile home on the property. His mother spent a lot of time with him, but most of the time she stayed with us to help with Todd. Clyde and Nita were running the liquor store and spending most of their time together.

Todd, Stacy and I were active in church, but I felt like I didn't have a life myself. I couldn't see a future for me. *There's got to be more,* I thought. I felt I needed a job — not only to have something to do while the kids were in school — but I needed the money. It couldn't be a full time job, but I needed something. Then it dawned on me. *I'm really good with hair,* I thought. *I'll go to beauty school!*

I decided I could put a shop right in my home, then I could be at home for Todd. After all, I had plenty of business experience with my Merle Norman Studios — going to beauty school and setting up a home business wouldn't be that hard for me to do. Also, there would be people around to

99

TODD...

talk to and I would once again have the finances to take care of us. It would be perfect!

"I want to go, too," Laverne said enthusiastically, when I shared my plan with her.

Laverne and I put in our applications for beauty school, and soon we were enrolled and making the forty-five minute trip together to school, five days a week. The round trips were never dull as we chattered excitedly, never running out of things to talk about. And at the school, we became the life of the party. Laverne, at thirty-six and I, at forty-two, were much older than the other girls, but we managed to keep them in stitches while we took care of more customers than any of them.

Going forward with my plan for a business, I asked Clyde for money to close the bays of our three car garage and to make it into a hair salon. Clyde did give me the money and I turned that garage into a very beautiful salon, complete with a shower for Todd. Now he would no longer just have a sponge bath, but a real shower! I never did get my beauty license (as you'll see later on), but that garage became a refuge for me and I cut an awful lot of free hair for Todd and his friends and my neighbors.

LAVERNE MORRIS AND I HAD SUCH A WONDERFUL FRIENDSHIP!

Laverne and her boys spent a lot of time at our house. Mamaw was a tremendous help, but somehow having someone with us who was not family made a difference, and all of us, Laverne and her boys, Todd, Stacy, Mamaw and I, became one big family.

Laverne was good with Todd, but he still wanted only me to do things for him. An intercom had been installed in Todd's room, which was on one end of our big sprawling house, and one in my room located on the other end. I was a light sleeper, and at night, the slightest sound from the speaker would bounce me right out of bed. One night, I jumped out of bed, and, in the darkness headed for the door I always kept open, and... Wham! My face ran painfully into the door that had somehow gotten closed.

"I heard Todd call you," Laverne said the next morning. "Then I heard you hit the door, but I knew you were all right when I heard you mumbling to yourself going down the hall."

She said she realized at that moment how really committed I was to Todd. She also realized how very difficult it was for me and encouraged me to reach out for a life of my own — to let go a little and allow my family to assume some responsibility. I had always felt I didn't have a choice, that everything depended on me. Laverne helped me see how bound up in my children I had become.

I knew she was right. There were times when I was irritable with Todd, when I was just so tired I could hardly put one foot in front of the other. I remembered the talk I had given Todd when he was discouraged because he thought he would never be able to have fun again.

Suddenly, I realized we needed to have fun again — I needed to have fun again. Life for my family was becoming more normal. We were moving into a time when things were getting easier emotionally — we could let our guard down a little and not be afraid to trust the future. We could have fun.

Halloween was almost upon us and Laverne and I decided we would have a party for the kids. We had a ball getting things ready for a wiener roast and all kinds of activities.

We worked hard cleaning our huge yard. I'd had some work done on it, even having a path paved down to the pond for Todd. The pond was his favorite place, but it was also the place where his usual good nature gave way to some of his darkest moods.

Todd and Stacy spent a lot of time by the pond talking, sharing their teenage secrets. In time, Stacy shared one of those secrets with me.

"Mom, I was so worried about Todd one day down by the pond," she remembered. "The water was so calm and peaceful and I was feeling good being there with Todd — then he started saying things that scared me." Stacy's eyes misted, as she went on.

"Todd said, '*You know, Stace, sometimes I sit here and see the water like it is now, and I think it wouldn't be so bad to die.*' I thought he just meant when the time came, but he said, '*No, I mean right now, in the water. It would be so easy. I could just roll down to the edge and just keep on going.*' He scared me talking like that.

"At first I thought he was teasing me, but I saw the look on his face, he meant it. I knew I ought to tell you right away but he made me promise not to say anything."

It was times like that I realized how hard our life had been for my lovely daughter Stacy.

The day of the party, the weather was perfect and our place looked beautiful. Fifty kids and grown-ups showed up. One of the deacons from our church even brought his tractor and a trailer loaded with hay for a hay ride. It was a fantastic party.

Todd really shined, feeling very much like part of the group. One of the things that worried Todd was the way people stare at the handicapped, but I had told him they do that because they feel uncomfortable, they simply don't know how to respond.

"Todd," I told him. "Just for that reason you have to give one hundred-and-fifty percent of yourself. You have to make people know you are okay with yourself and with your wheelchair. Make them know you're glad to be alive and able to be in that chair."

He seemed to understand and it was obvious from the way he behaved around everyone at the party, that Todd really did enjoy life. Todd also had a way of making people feel at ease around him. It was amazing, he couldn't even bait a hook, but he could teach a person how to fish. That afternoon, he was right there in the middle of the fishing and the paddle boating — even though he could only sit on the pier and watch.

I was very proud of Todd that day. As he mingled with the crowd, everyone could tell that he was comfortable with himself.

It was encouraging that he was not relying solely on me anymore, but I was still taking care of his personal needs, and there were times when I became very weary and wished we could get someone to take over so I could just be his mom.

Todd never resented his wheelchair, in fact he seemed to enjoy it. He drove me crazy racing around in that thing, even wanting a chair that would go faster. I was concerned though, because he fought being strapped into his chair. Todd didn't feel handicapped and hated being treated like he was.

Todd was still growing, so about every six to eight months we had to buy him another chair to keep up with his growth. Once when a new chair was delivered, the delivery man cautioned Todd —

"Remember, Todd," he said. "This chair goes faster than your old one. You'll have to be careful and always be buckled in."

The afternoon sun was hot, but Todd wanted to try out his new chair. Mamaw moved the van out of the way so Todd would have all the concrete to see what his chair would do. He tore out across the yard and hit a bump and went leaping out of that chair. For a moment, as he flew through the air, it seemed that his whole body was working. He appeared to jump up and out of the chair, his arms and legs in motion, then he landed face down on the grass.

When Mamaw got out of the van and saw Todd, she almost had a heart attack, but when she saw me doubled up laughing, and Todd lying flat on his face laughing too, she calmed down.

Todd wasn't hurt, but the problem was — how were we going to get this two hundred sixty pound, six-foot-three inch guy who was lying flat on his face on the ground, back in his chair. Of course we did it, but from that day on, Todd always had us buckle him in.

TODD... MY SON

ME IN MY OFFICE PAYING BILLS — WHY IS THIS SIGNIFICANT? BECAUSE I WAS NOW RESPONSIBLE FOR OUR HOUSEHOLD AND HAD TO MAKE IT WORK!

CHAPTER 16
2 YEARS — CAREERS

With our big Halloween party over, the rest of the year slipped by. The Christmas holidays came and Clyde even joined us — we had finally reached the point where we could be civil to each other and friendly. After the holidays, Todd and Stacy went back to school.

Laverne and I were doing pretty well in the beauty school we were attending, but there was a lot of pressure. One of the school rules was that if anyone were late for school beyond the specified check-in time, they would not be given credit for that day.

Because of my separation from Clyde, the ability to make money had become prominent in my mind. I felt that my completing beauty school was so important to our financial future, that I had made a commitment to myself to be in school no matter what happened at home.

One day I overslept and Laverne was late getting to my house to ride with me. I was in a quandary. I could either get Todd up and dressed and be late for school (and be counted as absent for the day), or I could get dressed myself and leave Todd in bed all day until I got in at four o'clock. He told me to go ahead and go to school, assuring me he would be alright.

"I love you, Mama," Todd called after me as I headed to my room to get dressed.

How stupid, I scolded myself. *It's silly for me to let Todd lie in bed all day just because I want to be counted. It isn't fair,* I thought. *I can't stand this pressure any longer.*

I was trying so hard to make everything work — to get the education I needed to support my family and allow me the freedom I needed. But I knew there must be another way. There was no way I would leave Todd in bed all day just to be counted at beauty school. No way.

I decided to drop out of the school even though the instructors were understanding and willing to work with me. Laverne left with me. Later we enrolled in a beauty college closer to Emory — once again the oldest ones there, and once again the life of the party. School was completely separate from my life at home, and the laughter was healing for me.

Mamaw stayed with Todd during the day, did the cooking, and fed him, but she and I found ourselves locked in a battle over what Todd should eat. I was determined Todd was going to eat sensibly so he would not gain weight. Mamaw, in her typically grandmotherly way, would cook anything he wanted and spoiled him as she had always done. Todd needed to take responsibility for himself so he could have a good life, but he found it enjoyable being spoiled by his grandmother. Clyde also felt that Todd should have whatever he wanted. He felt that with everything Todd had gone through, giving in to a few whims wouldn't hurt him.

This was a struggle that wasn't easily resolved.

THERE WAS A HUGE ADJUSTMENT WHEN TODD CAME HOME,
BUT WE GOT THROUGH IT — AND LIVED WELL

CHAPTER 17
TODD'S FUTURE

Todd surprised us all when he became interested in singing. Todd had sung in the church choir in Emory before his accident, but we were told he would not be able to sing because he had no control over his diaphragm. He was not supposed to even be able to breathe, much less sing! But Todd would not give up the idea of singing.

One day a man came into the beauty school for a hair cut. Jimmy Gilbert was an insurance salesman, but had at one time been a minister and missed it. Jimmy heard Laverne and I talk about Todd and how he wanted to sing. He thought he might be able to help him with his dream of singing and asked to meet him.

I knew Todd would be furious if I asked a stranger to our home to help him with singing, so Jimmy and I decided that he should come and tell us about the insurance policies he offered.

Jimmy came to our home, and after listening to his spiel, I did buy some insurance — not because I would feel less deceptive, but because he'd convinced me that I actually did need insurance in case something happened to me — my family needed to be taken care of. Jimmy also gave me some very shocking statistics. He said according to insurance companies' statistics, the usual life of a quadriplegic is seven years.

I had thought I was prepared for anything, but suddenly I felt as if someone reached out with a knife and cut away years that I had counted on. Sure Todd was having a rough time now — but I always believed he would someday have a life of his own, independent of me, with a wife and even children.

This jolt to my faith was a little more than I could handle. Jimmy Gilbert, who still had the heart of a minister, talked and prayed with us until the shock he'd given melted into a peaceful calm. We had to believe that God was in control and everything was going to be all right.

That afternoon with Jimmy Gilbert was a turning point for Todd. He became very serious about singing and began practicing diligently. An excellent singer, Jimmy offered Todd some good tips.

Laverne who had a beautiful voice and had been singing all her life also started helping him. She'd write the words to songs on paper and hang them around in his room that he was also using for a studio. She was amazed at Todd's feel for the music and the mechanics of singing since he had never had any training at all.

Todd had gained enough movement in his shoulder that, with a ratchet on his left hand, he had enough control to punch his practice cassette on and off. This gave him the independence to practice when no one was there to help him.

I felt there was something more going on with Todd than just singing for his pleasure, but was dumfounded when he announced he wanted to do a special for church.

When the day came for Todd to sing, I was nervous — almost to the point of nausea, but he didn't seem at all nervous. The pastor asked me to come forward to introduce my son, and I told a little bit about Todd, and then introduced him. I adjusted the microphone to the proper height for him, and he just wheeled right up to the front of the church, turned his chair around and faced the congregation with a big smile on his face.

With complete confidence, Todd looked directly into the eyes of the congregation and as the backup tape began to play, Todd sang *He Chose Me* without missing a cue.

There was not one person that day who wasn't touched by his song. Todd didn't have a great singing voice, but he had a lot of charisma. I sat in awe of this son of mine and was very proud.

Todd added more songs to his repertoire, and began singing in public often. As he sang at other churches and for happenings like "Youth For Christ," he would completely captivate his audience.

One night I was jarred out of bed by the intercom.

"Mom! Mom! Come here quick!"

I never got used to that intercom. Not only was it hard on the nervous system, but I think subconsciously, there was always the fear that Todd could be sick. I stumbled down the long hall between our rooms.

"Hurry, Mama," said Todd urgently. "Get a pencil and paper."

I rushed to Todd's desk and got paper and pencil. I knew by the tone of his voice that this had to be important.

"Mom, write this down...

I was lying flat on my back,
No where else to look but up,
When Jesus said, "Follow Me.
I had nothing more to lose,
When Jesus said, "Follow Me."

"Mom, that's good. Huh?"

Tears splashed onto the paper as I wrote down what he'd said.

Todd was excited because this was an insert for the song *He Chose Me*. I believe that Jesus dropped that verse into Todd's spirit in the middle of the night that night. From then on when Todd sang that song, it had new meaning for both of us.

I was always nervous when Todd sang. My heart would turn over but Todd would be as calm as if he had sang all his life. There was truly an anointing on his voice. The words of one song in particular slid deep into my heart and has come back to comfort me many times.

"Because He lives, I can face tomorrow.
Because He lives, all fear is gone.
Because I know He holds the future,
My life is worth the living
Just because He lives.

And then one day I'll cross that river,
And fight life's final war with pain
And then as death gives way to victory
I'll see the lights of Glory
And I'll know He reigns"

We didn't know that when Todd sang this song by Bill and Gloria Gaither, he was singing his destiny. It was a good time in our lives. We had been through some pretty tough times, but now we felt we were in God's special plan for our lives. Todd had heard from God, and he was doing what he felt God wanted him to do. There was joy as there always is in obedience. We had walked through pain, but in that walk, we became stronger.

We had so much fun as we traveled from place to place for Todd to sing. Once, to a big church in Dallas, then on to Greenville. He was at ease as he sang before hundreds of people.

At first, I would introduce him and his song, then he began doing it all himself. He enjoyed speaking to all those people, and it served tremendously to build his self-confidence.

TODD AND TONI QUIZAR

CHAPTER 18
RISE AND WALK — MAYBE

Having accepted his limitations, Todd was getting on with his life. No one who was close to him ever stopped believing that there would — someday — be something to help him walk.

One of his coaches encouraged him to go to Miami to a research center that works with patients with spinal cord injuries. They would evaluate Todd's injury and try to find a way to help him walk. Todd agreed to go if I could go with him.

We had not had any kind of vacation since the accident, so we decided to go. We'd have fun while we found out if there was any hope for Todd. Pecos Douglas, the brother of a friend of mine, offered us the use of his condominium in Destin, Florida.

That decided us. We'd go.

Next we needed to decide who would make the trip with us.

Number one on our list was Toni Quizar, a girl who had visited Todd while he was in Dallas Rehab. I knew that since she and Todd had started going together in their junior year, that Toni was very special to Todd. They seemed to be very much in love.

Laverne and her two boys, Mark and Little Todd would go, as well as Stacy and her friend Amy.

I insisted that everyone get a good night's sleep before leaving on the sixteen hour trip to our first destination — but Todd could not settle down, so we just loaded up the van at three in the morning and headed out.

We had borrowed a rooftop luggage carrier, but one of the boys had run the van through an automatic car wash and lost it. So we had to rent a trailer for our luggage. We must have been a strange sight when we stopped at the condominium that was to be our home for the next few days.

Everyone was weary, but the exhaustion we felt almost disappeared when we saw our temporary home with its three bedrooms, sunken tub, glass walls, plus a fantastic view of the ocean. I will always be grateful to Pecos Douglas, the man with a big heart, who loaned us his place for a whole week. We had a terrific time.

We drove from Destin to the Orlando airport to pick up Todd's coach who was flying down to be with Todd. None of us had ever been to Florida, and we wanted to enjoy every minute. We got rooms at the Polynesian Hotel at Disney World, and from there we set out to have fun. Disney World is completely handicap accessible — also with Todd along, we got in all the lines first and got special attention at the shows. It was great.

We found everything so easy, we decided to split up instead of being one group. Todd and Toni wanted to be alone, but I had been too long Todd's protector, so I insisted I go with them — I was afraid Toni would not be able to handle Todd's chair. I discreetly stayed far enough behind so they would have some privacy. They were so cute together.

One day while we were there, we had a downpour and everyone started running for cover. Before I could get to Todd and Toni, I saw Toni hop on the back of Todd's chair, wrap her arms around his neck while Todd headed for cover. I just stood there in the drenching rain, watching. I saw my son and the woman he loved dealing with a situation by themselves. In Toni's eyes Todd was a man and she trusted him to take care of her, and he did.

Todd insisted on wearing shorts like the rest of the kids. I couldn't help but laugh the first time I put a pair on him, but his big hairy lifeless legs were no problem for him, he was one of the gang. Todd had made a great discovery on this trip, control of his life was in his hands. He felt capable — and he was.

We left for Miami at five in the morning. Todd, Toni, his coach and I were making the trip. (With all the driving we were doing, we were beginning to think this little state was as big as Texas, at least in length, and we found the tall palms and citrus trees fascinating.)

We reached Miami at noon, and after several stops to ask directions, we found the Spinal Cord Research Center. The center, located in a huge hospital complex, had been established by a football player and his dad. The athlete had been in an accident that paralyzed him, and he worked diligently to strengthen his body to ready himself for the spinal cord cure.

I was disappointed because Todd wasn't that interested in the same thing. He had become satisfied where he was physically, and he had more or less come to Miami to humor me. I had tried everything I knew to try, bought books written by people who had the same injury as Todd, tried to interest him in handicap games, but Todd was happy as he was.

Maybe, I thought. *He's afraid nothing will work.*

But Todd really was content physically. He didn't need help, he just wanted to be left alone. But since he wanted to please his coach and me, he'd agreed to go through with the tests.

We spent the day talking to many therapists, and they all agreed that Todd was a good candidate for the "Miami Project," as their program was called.

"Since Todd hasn't had any corrective surgery," they told us. "We feel he can benefit from our program."

We learned that Todd would have to wait another year until he would be eighteen, then he could come to Miami to live with an aide. He would be put through a rigorous program designed to stimulate muscles to try to get back some of their movement.

I was very encouraged and felt like we were headed for something great. To my surprise, Todd was not impressed.

"Todd, you could act a little more enthusiastic," I scolded. "I'm disappointed in you. This is your body we're talking about."

"Yes, it is my body," he answered quietly.

I felt this could really be a chance for Todd to regain some, if not all, use of his body, but it was as though Todd was thinking,

"Well, Mom, I've come down here and done what you wanted — now maybe you'll leave me alone for awhile."

We left Miami after all the evaluations and meetings a little subdued and anxious to get back to Orlando where the others were waiting — though not impatiently. They had enjoyed another day at Disney World, and their jubilance lifted our spirits as we treated ourselves to a nice dinner. We had a long trip ahead of us the next day. Home was waiting.

Todd and I had no chance at all on the trip to talk privately, so it was good, after getting home, to be able to share about the trip. I was a little hesitant to ask him about his relationship with Toni, but Todd laughed, and said, unashamedly,

"If it could have been any better being normal, I don't know how I could have stood it."

I cried for him. A wife and children really would not be out of the realm of possibilities. Not letting myself wonder about this situation too much, I was glad for Todd that his life seemed to finally be normal, whatever, that meant. I had worked so hard to help Todd be as independent as he possibly could, and now for the first time since his accident, I felt he really would have a future. And, maybe I could have one, too.

TODD AT DISNEY WORLD... WHAT A GREAT TIME WE HAD THERE

CHAPTER 19
4 YEARS — SENIOR YEAR

Summer quickly passed and the kids began their yearly ritual of looking for new clothes that would attract attention while making sure they would fit in. Todd would begin his senior year, but he was not too interested in getting his diploma, he just wanted to be with his friends.

"Todd, we've worked too hard for you to just throw it away," I grumbled.

I harped on the subject until he got mad, but I remembered the struggle he went through every day to go to school and how hard it was on me to dress him just right day after day, padding his shoulders so they wouldn't show their deterioration. I longed to see him in his cap and gown in the line of excited graduates waiting to move up to that podium to get his diploma. Even with all my harping, I didn't feel I was making much headway with him until he didn't get the letter he was expecting. The high school sent out letters to all the seniors to advise them that they would be getting senior pictures made. Todd didn't get a letter.

"Mama, call the school," he insisted. "Find out why I didn't get my letter." He might not have wanted that diploma, but he wanted the recognition that would show he was included with his class.

"Mrs. Odom," said the counselor. "Todd isn't going to be able to graduate with his class, he doesn't have enough credits."

Todd was incensed. His whole attitude changed from "I don't care," to "just let them try to stop me!" He was going to graduate with his class — no matter what it took.

"It's going to take a lot of work," the principal told us. "Todd, you'll have to take a full load, not just half a day this year."

First, we had his picture taken for the yearbook — just like the rest of the senior class. Then there was the problem of finding an aide who would stay with him all day, every day, writing for him, feeding him, doing all the things he could not do for himself.

Laverne volunteered. Laverne was a good friend, but this was asking a lot. But she was insistent.

"I can do it," Laverne offered. "I want to apply for the job."

I was overjoyed. I knew Laverne would be a great motivator for Todd, and if anyone could pull this off, she could.

Laverne took Todd to school for pep rally day just before school started. I had things to do at home, so I didn't go, but the phone rang, and one of the counselors at school said,

"Terry, Laverne said to tell you to come down to the school."

I wondered why, but I didn't argue — you never knew with Todd when he might really need me.

Laverne acted nonchalant when I got there.

"I just thought you should be here."

It didn't take much to figure that something was going on — so I sat beside Laverne on one of the hard backless bleachers and waited as the excitement mounted. The pep rally began with the invocation and who should come rolling his chair onto the gymnasium floor but Todd, where he prayed, asking God for guidance during the coming year, for his team and classmates.

It was hard to believe. I remembered back to Todd's time in Dallas Rehab — he'd been so introverted. Now, here he was before his whole school leading the invocation.

You've come a long way, Todd, I said to myself and wiped away the tears.

The pep rally began with a *Rah! Rah! Rah!* and a lot of yelling and jumping cheerleaders. The coaches, one by one, gave their speeches to motivate their team to be a winner this year. Head Coach Brandon finished his speech with:

"Now, we have a special honor we'd like to give for this coming year. We met before the rally and decided that we want Todd Odom to be one of our teammates. We all agreed that if not for his wheelchair, Todd would be on our team today. So we would like to give him the honor of being a member of the Wildcat team this year."

The band came to life and the boys came running into the gym, with Todd, in his Wildcat jersey, leading the pack. Through my tears, I saw a grin on Todd's face as big as Texas. The stadium erupted into wild cheers and applause as the band played, spurring the team on to be winners. I could not guess what was in the hearts of the rest of the team, but I knew what was in the heart of their newest team member — he definitely felt like a winner.

As the pep rally ended, the football team circled the gym, following Todd in his chair. They circled the floor again and again, closing into a spiral, with Todd in the center.

When I heard the *Hoot! Hoot! Hoot!* of the team, it was overwhelming. Then I saw Todd head his chair toward Laverne and me as the rally broke up. He rolled up and just looked up at me with that big smile. We didn't need words.

Before every football game that year, the pep rally was led by Todd. At one special pep rally, he even made the speech. I watched the kids around Todd, and I felt they treated him no different than anyone else. Often, one would even jump on the back of his chair and hitch a ride, but they always seemed to have respect and honor for him.

Regretfully, Todd and Toni had broken off their relationship soon after our trip to Florida, and he began dating one of the Tigerettes. He certainly had a way with girls, she was devoted to him like Toni was, maybe even more so.

He went to all the games that year, at home or away. We would load him in the van that was painted with bright colored slogans, and with streamers flying, we would get behind the bus load of kids, and away we would go. Todd would be waiting as the kids would get off the bus, then during the game he'd roll his chair up and down the sidelines. But in his mind he was not on the sidelines, he was in the game with his team mates as he watched every move they made.

My greatest fear during those times was that Todd would somehow be knocked over in his chair and be hurt or humiliated, that people would see just how really vulnerable and helpless Todd was. But I was the one who suffered the humiliation.

It happened during a game in Brownsboro, Texas. We were in a big rock stadium that had a rock fence separating the stands from the playing field. During one of the plays, some of the players ran toward the sideline right where Todd was and before he could get out of the way, they ran right over him. He wasn't knocked out of his chair or hurt, but when I saw those big football players heading non-stop toward my son, I leaped from my seat and cleared that rock fence.

Todd was laughing, feeling very much a part of the game, having been tackled, but I had to be helped up from where I was sprawled on the ground — I almost broke my leg. After that, I didn't worry so much about Todd.

Those were exciting times and we felt blessed to be part of them. Because of Coach Brandon, Todd was able to participate in one of the most important things in his life.

TODD ON THE FIELD WITH HIS TEAM — THE RAINES WILDCATS

CHAPTER 20
ERIC

Another Halloween was approaching, and remembering how much fun our party was last year, Laverne and I decided to have another one. We felt Todd would have even more fun at this one because he was so much more involved in life than this time the year before. And besides — we were all hilariously happy for a change.

"Mama," Todd said to me once. "People think that we shouldn't be happy, but we really are happy."

We laughed, knowing we had a secret most people didn't know. — the Lord had taught us many things about being happy, even when things look impossible. It was almost like our close little family group was in a happy conspiracy, but we were ready to share our secret anytime we had a chance. I was soon to be put to the test, about sharing more than the secret, with a boy named Eric.

Todd had slowed down with his singing and it concerned me a little, but he was so busy with his studies and extra things he was involved in, he just didn't have time.

"Mama, guess what? I got a part in a play," he came home one day and told me. The part was that of a computer whiz in the school play. Stacy also had a part playing a part, an athlete named "Babushka".

Todd and Eric McKinney, a boy in the drama class, were becoming pals. Todd had always had a lot of friends, but since the accident, he hadn't really had a close male friend, one he could share male things with. I knew he and Eric had both become close, but one day they threw me for a loop.

"Mama," Todd began. "We were wondering, would you care if Eric moves in with us?"

Eric nervously put his hands in his pockets, not saying anything.

"He's not happy at home, Mama, and he sure needs a place to stay. He could pay rent — he works at Piggly Wiggly." Todd was giving it his best shot. "He'd even help you around the house."

"Todd, I don't know."

Todd thought I would be an easy mark if he asked in front of Eric, but I wasn't sure this would be a good idea.

"I'll think about it." But, as soon as Eric left, I told Todd how I really felt. "Todd, there's no way I'll let this happen. I've got all I can do to take care of you and Stacy. Eric would be another mouth to feed and another responsibility for me, somebody else to wait on. No way, Todd."

"Mom, I promise you won't have to wait on Eric, he'll help you," Todd pleaded. "He even said he'd get me up."

"He hasn't seen you get up yet, Todd." I argued.

"But, Mama..." Todd said.

"The answer is no, Todd. The subject is closed."

I left the room before we really got into it.

Todd and Eric's friendship grew.

"Mom, I forgot how good it is to have a guy to talk to."

Todd was enjoying having a close friend. He seemed to have forgotten our disagreement about Eric moving in with us or so I thought. One night we had a big fight. The fact that Todd was only seventeen and in a wheelchair didn't mean we didn't fight. That night I was furious with him. I began unbuckling his restraining belt so I could get him out of his chair. I gritted my teeth as I took his chair down then slipped the body jacket off his hulking frame. His tee shirt came off next, then I had to strip down the chair and put the belt back on him and tighten it and get ready to do the lift, which was used to get him into bed. Our bedtime ritual was going smoothly, but my temper was anything but smooth. After Todd was in bed, I told Stacy,

"I've got to get out of here for awhile."

By the time I got in my car I was crying out loud. It was ten thirty when I headed from our house in the country. Caring for someone who is completely helpless sometimes takes it's toll. I was so weary, and I needed someone to talk to who would understand. I automatically headed toward Laverne's house in Emory — I knew she'd understand. Laverne was asleep when I got there, but her boys let me in. When they saw my tears, they pointed me toward their mother's bedroom. She was sound asleep. There was laundry scattered all over one side of the bed, but I just raked it off onto the floor. She woke up when I plopped down on the side of the bed.

"What's wrong, friend?" Laverne asked sleepily as she rolled over and slowly raised up on one elbow.

"I've run away from home," I sobbed.

Laverne smiled indulgently, "You have?"

"Yes, I have. I just had to get away."

"Well, you know you can always run away from home to my house."

"I know," I said gratefully.

I really unloaded on Laverne that night. For hours she listened patiently to things she already knew — nothing new, just the same old things, but it felt good just to know someone cared. At twelve-thirty in the morning, I finally said,

"I've got to go back home."

Stacy was with Todd, so I wasn't worried about him, but I had never just up and left them before. But one thing I was sure of was that my children were responsible and could take care of themselves. Nevertheless, I left in a hurry to get back home.

When I turned into my drive, I saw we had company. Eric was there. He had run away from home, too — but he had run away to my house. He had moved in, lock, stock, and sneakers. Todd was very excited — he knew once the deed was done, he could get me to see their side of things.

"Okay, boys. We'll see how it works. We'll give it a try," I said. "But Eric, I'm not going to wait on you — you'll have to help."

Eric promised he would help me, and help me he did. I didn't realize how much Eric could help me, but in the days and weeks to come, my life took a drastic turn. Eric had his driver's license, and unlike Stacy, with only a hardship license, he could drive Todd anywhere. Stacy could only drive Todd to school, but Eric could drive him to the movies, on double dates, and into Emory where they would sit on the square and visit with the other kids. When that van rolled into town — it was social time.

When the van parked on the square, kids would surround it and visit for hours. Church activities were the only other recreation they had — unless one of them threw a party.

Suddenly, I found I could have a social life of my own. It had been four years since Todd's accident, and now I could actually go out and eat with friends. But I still enjoyed my kids.

The time finally came for the school play. I went to all three performances. I was so proud, not only of Todd and Stacy, but of Little Todd, Mark and Toni, who were also in the play. I kept hoping Todd and Toni would get back together, but it didn't happen. *[They had done a song together in drama class earlier in the year. The kids said it was a song about pledging their love to each other, but it had only been a song.]*

"This is almost unbelievable," I told the Lord, as I watched Todd come rolling out, as a computer whiz, wearing a long wig and sunglasses. He and Stacy both had speaking parts and I was so proud of them. God had been good to us — our lives, seeming so hopeless at times, were becoming normal and very, very happy.

Another Christmas was almost here. *How far we've come since the Christmas Todd was in Dallas Rehab and Clyde was in the hospital,* I thought.

The pressure was not as great anymore and usually things went pretty smooth, but once in awhile Todd and I would butt heads.

It was the night before Christmas Eve. I had begun to get Todd ready for bed, and he started smarting off to me as teenagers will do. My temper flared and I wasn't paying attention to what I was doing. As I started my lift, I didn't get my footing right. When I started lifting him into bed — we didn't make it.

There he was, sitting halfway between the chair and the bed. I needed him to be in the bed not halfway. I tried to realign myself, but when I lifted again, I felt my back pull. Todd and I both knew we were in trouble. Somehow, I managed to get him into bed, then I called Stacy to come and help me finish getting him settled in.

The pain in my back did not get better even with pain pills. The next morning Stacy had to lift Todd for me and together we got him ready for the day. I still felt I could manage the lifts and Todd's care if I would be very careful — it was Christmas and I didn't have time for this. Stacy wanted to spend Christmas Eve with my mother, as she and her cousin Tami usually did.

"Go ahead, Stacy," I insisted. "I'll be fine."

I thought if I was really careful, I could do it. Instead, I spent the rest of the holidays flat of my back in bed, unable to do anything for Todd or anyone else.

In a few days, I was in the hospital. For the first time since Todd's accident, he was having to do without me. For four years I had been the one to wipe his nose, feed him and bathe him, and do all the things his hands could not do. When I talked to him on the phone from the hospital, he would complain,

"Mama, when are you coming home? My hair looks awful."

He had learned to depend on me to make him look his best and he wanted to look good. He felt very good about himself, and had the charisma of his Dad. With Mamaw helping, Stacy was getting him up and off to school every morning. They were all doing well, except when they washed Todd's hair — they just washed it — when I was there, I took time to make it look good.

While this time of separation had been forced between Todd and me, it helped me to see that maybe Todd would be able to do without me some of the time. Maybe I could get a job, now that I knew he could survive without me.

When I came home from the hospital, I still couldn't do the things I had done for Todd. I still couldn't lift him, but I did do his hair. Eric took a big load off my shoulders. Young and strong, he could do the lifting for me.

ERIC

TODD... MY SON

SENIOR PROM

TODD AND KIM TRIPP
(RIGHT)

ERIC MCKINNEY AND
DELIA TUCKER
(TOP LEFT)

CHAPTER 21
PROM

The holidays had come and gone and school was beginning again. It seemed only yesterday that we were bringing Todd home from Dallas Rehab for his coming home party. Now, here we were, going into the last semester of his senior year. The days were flying by with school activities. Football was over but there was basketball and track.

However, Todd and Eric had begun to be interested in other things besides sports — girls. They spent most of their time with their heads together figuring out strategies for finding females.

As prom time approached Todd asked one of the most popular girls in his school to go and, to my excitement, she accepted.

How can I go about fitting him for a tuxedo? I wondered.

I found a store in Greenville and a nice lady named Melanie who told me exactly how to measure Todd, and we proceeded to order his tux.

However, things didn't go quite as planned. The afternoon of the prom, I picked up his tux. That evening, in order to dress Todd, I had to put him back into bed, but as I tried to put the tux on him, it wouldn't fit right. Todd was becoming more and more anxious as we struggled. Panic stricken, I called Melanie.

"What am I going to do?" I almost yelled.

Melanie asked for directions, then drove thirty-five miles to our house bringing everything we needed to get Todd's tux together.

God is so good. Melanie stayed with me until Todd and Eric left to pick up their girls for the prom. Oh, how exciting for me to watch as both boys left in their tuxes looking like they were worth a million dollars. Melanie and I stood in the drive with tears in our eyes, watching my son go off to the prom — just like everyone else.

Todd...

One day toward the end of the school year, Todd asked,

"Mom, can I have a party here at the house for the seniors?"

I thought, *Give 'em an inch and they take a mile.*

However, I thought it was a great idea. Todd couldn't go to many of their functions because of the lack of accessibility for his chair, but they could sure come to our house. Once again, preparations for a party — how wonderful! I was looking forward to another party, but Todd was feeling a little constricted.

"Mom, I wish you would go somewhere tonight. You're always watching over me, and I just want to be free to be me. Stacy'll be here to see that I'm all right."

I started to object.

"Mom, please," Todd said. "I'll be fine."

"Oh, all right, Todd," I said. "But I don't have anywhere to go." (It had been a long time since I'd had a social life.)

"Don't worry, Mama," Todd said, brightening. "I know a place up on the lake. I'll call my friend Ronnie and he'll meet you there. You know how you like to dance."

"Okay."

Playing the good sport, I agreed — I did love to dance. The night passed quickly and I had a really good time. And that night I met a red-bearded gentleman, Eddie Jones, who came over to the table where Ronnie and I were having dinner because he recognized that I was Todd's mom. Eddie talked with us for awhile but never mentioned dancing, so I said,

"Would you like to dance?" With only a hint of surprise, he bowed slightly and said,

"Sure, why not."

When I got home that night, there were kids everywhere. They assumed when they saw me, that they would have to go home, but I felt pretty good myself and I was just glad my kids were enjoying themselves. They had had so little joy the last few years and I knew they would outgrow this soon enough.

Eddie asked me to go dancing the very next weekend. It was fine with the kids, they wanted to have another party anyway. Eddie and I started going dancing every Friday night, then every Friday and Saturday night, then it was every Thursday, Friday and Saturday night. Eddie and I had a great time together and became good friends.

I had not dated since Clyde left and Eddie, a real gentleman, was the right person to help me begin that part of my new life. He would take me out to eat, then dancing — never putting pressure on me for anything more. I was beginning to feel like a woman again.

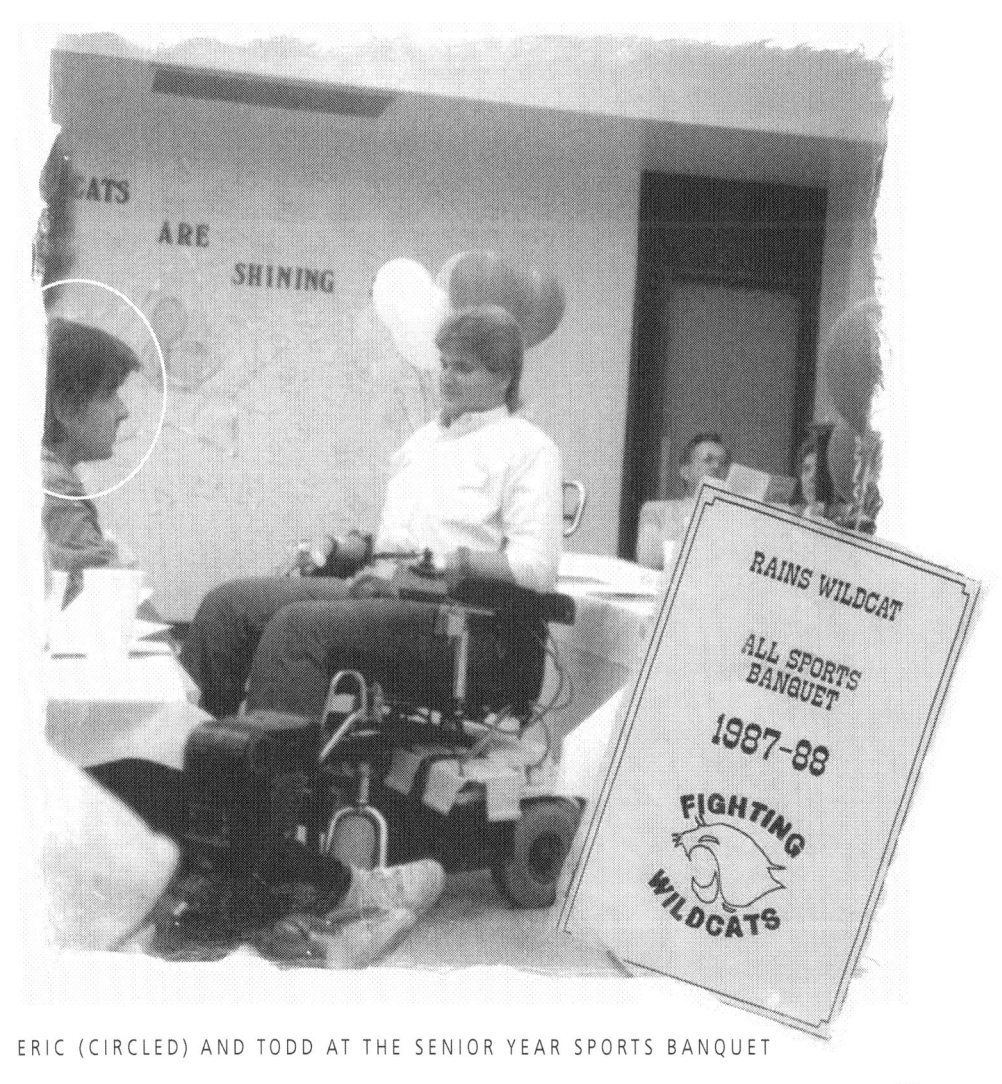

ERIC (CIRCLED) AND TODD AT THE SENIOR YEAR SPORTS BANQUET

GRADUATION WAS A MILESTONE COVERED ON THE LOCAL DALLAS NEWS

CHAPTER 22
GRADUATION

Graduation was getting close and Channel 8 News in Dallas wanted to do a story on Todd and film his whole graduation day. Reporter Matt Quinn and his television crew came to our house early that morning— then loaded up and followed Todd to school — filming the whole time.

They made Todd a star that day. They filmed conversations with the kids and teachers, the cafeteria length banana split that some of the mothers made for the seniors, and any of the seniors who wanted in on the action.

Later, exhausted, we all went home with cameras still rolling. Matt Quinn and I sat on the porch while he asked questions about our life after Todd was paralyzed. I experienced the feelings all over again as I remembered the pain and uncertainties of those months we spent in the hospital and then in Dallas Rehab. Again I felt the sinking feeling of disappointment as I told of time after time when our hopes for Todd's recovery were dashed. Finally, I was able to point to our life now and say, "But we made it."

Mark Morris, Laverne's son, and some of the other kids were interviewed, then Matt Quinn and the crew strolled down to the pier with Todd to hear him tell his own story.

That night, the graduation ceremony was wonderful. My family was there from Dallas and East Texas to see Todd graduate. I never really thought this day would come — when Todd would actually be in the line of graduates. But here it was — and there he was proudly rolling his chair up to receive his diploma.

After graduation, our house was abuzz with family and friends celebrating Todd's graduation, but mostly there to watch our story on the ten o'clock news. Every television set in the house was on — we didn't want to miss a scene. When the news came on, we impatiently waited through the news items that came up before our story. I was very excited, I felt good about my interview and thought that it would be a large part of the interview shown that night.

"After this," I bragged. "I'll probably be invited to the Oprah Winfrey Show."

"Shh... Here it is."

There was Todd getting ready to go to school, the kids at school talking about their relationship with Todd, and there was Todd's visit with Matt Quinn by the pier.

"Todd," Matt said. "With your handicap, what are some of the obstacles that keep you from doing what you want to do?"

Todd sat in silence for a few seconds.

"I don't see myself as handicapped," he finally answered. "I can do anything I want to — it's just a little harder for me than the other kids."

When the film was over, everyone clapped and cheered. We were all so proud of Todd, he was a real celebrity. He had come so far since 1985. The news team really did a thorough job, they even showed the banana split — But where was I? Where was that beautiful conversation I had with Matt Quinn? I couldn't believe it — and I thought I had done so well. *That's what you get for putting on airs!* I thought. *Oh well, I guess we can't all be stars.*

Todd truly was a star, he was voted "Best Personality" in his class, "Mr. R.H.S.," and he even received a letter in football.

I was so revved up from his success — that I became determined Todd should go on to college. ■

Mr. Raines High School — the highest honor the school bestowed.

NOW THAT HIGH SCHOOL GRADUATION WAS OVER,
I PUSHED TODD TO GO TO COLLEGE

CHAPTER 23
STACY

But college was the farthest thing from Todd's mind. He had found that he could have fun again, and fun was all he wanted.

Our house became the hangout for the kids of Emory. There was a party every Friday and Saturday night. My nerves were wearing very thin — there seemed no place for me to go to be alone. There were always people around everywhere. I wanted Todd to be popular and I wanted him to have fun, but he was becoming wilder and wilder. He had abandoned his music and quit going to church. I didn't like what was happening to my family. We were drifting farther and farther from our faith, the faith that had pulled us through so much. Eddie and I were still going dancing every weekend. All our lives seemed to be one long party.

Eric was still living with us, then Bradley moved in. Then came Brandon and Shaun. I began to feel that since Todd had so many people to take care of him, I could go to work.

Right before Todd's accident I had sold one of my Merle Norman Studios (although I had kept a 10% ownership) because Clyde thought I wasn't spending enough time with our family — the second one I sold before Todd actually came home to stay. Now, with all these people around helping Todd, I decided to take back my store in Terrell and get back to work and to my career. With these decisions made, I found myself spending less and less time with Stacy. Looking back, I find that I can't even remember much of her senior year — it's just a blur.

Our lives had changed so drastically — just one party after another — that we weren't even a family anymore. We began missing the way we were — even Todd was getting sick of all the parties.

Laverne and her boys were hardly ever around anymore since our lifestyle had changed so. Since Eddie was the friend I turned to now when I needed someone, Laverne and I lost the closeness we once had. Eddie was available to help my family when we needed something. He was also there for Todd for man talk or to fix his chair when it broke. Todd seemed happy with Eddie around, but I was concerned because things were getting out of hand between Eddie and me — after all I had been through with Clyde over the years, I was not ready for commitment from anyone.

I decided to rent an apartment in Terrell close to my Merle Norman studio — it would be a place to be alone. I spent two nights each week in Terrell, the other five nights I spent at home.

With the boys there, it was now easier for me to be away from Todd. I would arrange my days and nights so I could get Todd up one day, go to the studio, stay that night in my apartment, work the next day, come home and get Todd up in the early afternoon — only to start the routine over again.

The schedule I set for myself was hard on me and my nerves, but I felt I had to get my business off the ground again — we could not keep living on borrowed money. However, in all the shuffle, I was losing Stacy.

Stacy had always been in the honors program at school, but in her senior year her grades started falling and she became alienated from her schoolmates. One day when I came in for one of my nights home, I had a message from her principal asking me to bring Stacy to his office so we could talk.

The principal, Bob Clompton, was very kind as he spoke to us. He was a member of the church we had been attending, so he knew our situation and was very sympathetic to our needs. He knew how hard it had been on Stacy. He suggested that she drop the honors program because it was too rigid for her. Stacy had begun to hate school because it was so hard, and she had no problem dropping the honors program and entering the regular curriculum.

Stacy had also gotten a little wild in the partying atmosphere I'd allowed to be created at home. I had more or less turned my home over to Todd and his friends and they spent their time cooking, eating, drinking and partying. The late hours and the noise had kept Stacy from studying and, even worse, she had learned to join in.

While I was trying to get my Merle Norman business back off the ground and also trying to have a little social life of my own that was not totally wrapped up in my children, I had allowed communication between Stacy and myself to slide. But it still was a total surprise to me to find out that she had been cutting classes as well as even skipping whole days.

I felt like a failure. I knew I had to get back in touch with her, but I really didn't know how.

"Stacy we need to talk about this," I said. "I am so sorry I've put you in this position. What can I do to make it better for you?"

"Mama, I can't go to school and live in this house," Stacy sighed, her forehead creased in frustration.

"What do you want to do?" I asked, at a loss as to how to handle this new crisis in our lives.

"I think, maybe I should go live with Mamaw," she replied.

Stacy had always been level-headed and could always make good decisions, but I was dumfounded when she told me she wanted to go and live with Mamaw. I couldn't believe she meant it and it made me feel even more like a failure. I had been so careful to take care of Todd and not fail him that I had overlooked Stacy's needs. She had been my rock during the long months when I spent every minute with Todd — I could always count on Stacy being okay. Now, I learned that she was not okay. All that time, she had needed me, too. And I hadn't been there for her.

I really looked at my daughter — and what I saw hurt me. Stacy had been caught up in all the "good times" I had allowed to go on in our house and now she had no interest in school, her friends, or anything except having fun. It was as if she was trying to make up for the young years she had lost. I didn't know how to handle the problem and made an appointment to see her principal again to get some advice.

Stacy and I stopped in town to eat breakfast before our meeting with Bob Clompton. As I sat opposite Stacy in the restaurant, tears poured down my cheeks. I couldn't eat, I couldn't even swallow. It had been a long time since I had felt this helpless. I was still in tears as we talked with Bob and I admitted to him how miserably I had failed Stacy.

We were unable to come up with a solution that would keep her there, so I checked her out of school, wondering where it would all end. I agreed with Stacy that it would probably be better for her to move in with Mamaw, so we left the school and headed straight for Mamaw's — who we hadn't even asked if she would even allow Stacy to come and stay with her.

As I drove the forty-five miles to Clyde's mother's house, I remembered when I had left home at the age of sixteen and went to live with my aunt and uncle — I'd never felt I'd had a home until I married Clyde. The closer Stacy and I got to Mamaw's, the more convinced I was that this was not the right thing to do.

I can't do this, I cried to myself. *I can't lose Stacy.*

Stacy was my responsibility and I couldn't let her live with someone else, even someone as close to us as Mamaw. I didn't want her to leave me. An idea began forming in my mind. I wouldn't tell her she couldn't move in with Mamaw, but maybe I could get her to come and live with me in Terrell. At least she would still be with her mother — it's what I would have wanted when I was sixteen and found myself on my own.

"Stacy," I said. "You know, Mamaw is quite a bit older than me and she thinks differently. She loves you, but you might not be able to do some of the things you do living with me."

She looked at me questioningly.

"You'll be living in the country," I continued. And you won't have a car to run around in, so you won't be able to go to the mall and things like that very often."

I even went out of my way to drive by the school she would attend, a very small rural school, so she could compare it to the one she now attended. I painted a pretty bleak picture of what her life would be like and could tell she was thinking seriously about her decision.

"Stacy, I have an idea," I said. "You could move into my apartment in Terrell. You'd have time for yourself, and you and I could be together. How does that sound?"

I glanced over at her hopefully. I knew she needed to be away from the home atmosphere I had created for Todd, but I knew she still needed me and I needed her. I was relieved when she agreed that it was a good idea. Mamaw also felt we were making a wise choice under the circumstances.

I was relieved and I knew Stacy would be glad, too, once she was enrolled in school. She had attended school in Terrell until she was in the sixth grade, and she would be able to renew some friendships there. We drove over right away and got Stacy settled in my apartment.

I started staying four nights in Terrell with Stacy, then three nights in Emory with Todd. I had thought things were going to be easier since I didn't have to spend all my time with Todd, but I was now stretching myself even more to cover two homes — I was living two lives. The boys that were living at my house with Todd were taking good care of him, but I still took care of his personal needs. I still bathed him and did his hair.

I found I could manage pretty well splitting my week between my children. I was stretched pretty thin, trying to be what Todd wanted me to be and also what Stacy wanted me to be, but everything was working out just fine — or so I thought.

The third day of school, my sweet level-headed daughter rebelled. She refused to go to school or even to get out of bed. Finally, I yanked the pillow from under her head. She grabbed it and buried her head under it.

"Dang it, Stacy," I yelled. "Get out of that bed! That's all you ever want to do is sleep."

She just groaned and burrowed deeper under her pillow.

"Stacy, if you don't go to school, you'll have to go to the doctor," I threatened.

She did not cooperate, and we had a bang up good fight. I was very angry with her, but all I could do was go to work and leave her there.

Where have I failed?

I anguished all day, not knowing what to do. When I walked through the door that evening and saw Stacy, I knew we had to do something.

She sat curled up on the couch, desolate and beat down. She looked very frail and unhappy. I just crossed the room and sat down beside her taking her on my lap and rocking her like I did when she was a little girl. My seventeen year old daughter sat on my lap, her head on my shoulder and we both cried.

"Stacy," I said. "I want you to be happy, but I can't let you quit school. You have to graduate."

"Maybe if I moved in with Daddy," she said. "That might work. Then I could go back to school at Emory and be with my friends. Mom, it's my senior year! I just don't fit in with these kids. It's been too long, they don't really remember me and I don't remember them. I'm miserable!"

I hated the idea of her living with her dad. I really beat myself up, feeling like a failure. But we had tried this set-up and it hadn't worked. Reluctantly I said okay.

We called Clyde and he agreed to let Stacy move in with him. We moved her to her daddy's house that day. I felt like I had been through a wringer and I knew Stacy felt the same. But we had to do what was best for Stacy.

After Stacy left the apartment, I felt too lonely to stay there anymore. My relationship with Eddie had cooled somewhat — there was too much going on in my life — but he did help me move back to Emory. And in a few weeks Stacy was back home with the boys and me, staying with her father hadn't worked out either.

However, I was not really happy. My family wasn't happy. Finally it dawned on me that we were not living by faith anymore.

CHAPTER 24
GETTING OUR FAITH BACK ON TRACK

Things in our home had changed drastically since I had allowed Todd's friends to move into my house. They had gotten out of hand and their drinking was getting heavier and heavier. I tried to keep a tighter reign on them, but they were pretty hard to control. When the boys were drinking, they didn't take care of Todd as they should. The one exception was a young man named Jimbo.

Jimbo and Todd had become great friends and I could depend on him. However, Jimbo too was tired of the partying life we'd all fallen into and he wanted to get his life together. For that to happen, he felt he had to get away from Emory and the parties. Soon Jimbo left for California to try to do just that. But he was still concerned for Todd who was still right in the middle of all the partying. He called him a few times, telling him how great California was for the handicapped.

"Man, you oughta come out here — it's something else."

Todd started dreaming of a life in California. I knew he couldn't move there on his own, but I had always encouraged Todd to believe he could do anything he wanted — now he was ready to try something different. The more I thought about California and Todd leading an independent life, the more interesting it sounded. Maybe something could be worked out. Maybe it would be just what Todd needed to get him on the right track. I was also allowing myself to dream, but maybe it was not so far fetched.

One day not long after, I got a phone call from an old friend.

"Terry, do you remember how you always used to talk about working for the corporate offices of Merle Norman Cosmetics? Well, the job you wanted as a representative is available."

She gave me Merle Norman's phone number and encouraged me to call their vice president, Richard McClellan, for an interview. The job I would be applying for was in my own home state of Texas. With their home office in California, I'd be able to see Todd.

Amazed, I wondered if this could be an answer to prayer, or just a coincidence? Maybe the Holy Spirit was working again in our lives. Maybe this would be another milestone for us.

The kids were eager for me to call Mr. McClellan, so I called and he interviewed me over the phone. I got a call later asking me to fly to Los Angeles for a personal interview. I felt good about the job, thinking it was really a godsend. I called Jimbo, and we made arrangements for me to drive the ninety miles to his house during the week I would be in Los Angeles so we could talk about getting Todd out there.

However, the job opportunity was not for my home state of Texas, but New York. Todd, Stacy and I talked it over as a family and since Todd was already set on moving to California, I knew that I could work in New York and travel to California when needed and still come home to Stacy. But, as it always happens in God's plan — I had not been in California with the corporation for more than two days when I interviewed with a lovely woman named Darlene who asked why I would want to work in New York when I lived in Texas? I said that it was because New York was the only area open, but I'd love to work near my home. Wouldn't you just know that between the time I was to go to California for the interview with Richard McClellan, the position in New York was filled and one in Texas had opened up. That's when I knew that God had not left me.

Leaving Stacy with Todd and the boys at my house, I flew to Los Angeles, interviewed for the job and was hired on the spot. Jimbo and I then went apartment hunting where he lived south of Los Angeles and found just the one — an apartment that would accommodate Todd's chair. I contacted a doctor who agreed to take care of Todd's medical problems and an aide who would stay with Todd.

With new hope in my heart, I flew back home. It seemed we were always taking a few steps forward then a few steps back, but we always ended up just a little further ahead than we were and a little stronger.

It was two weeks before Christmas when we began making preparations for my training and Todd's move to California. We were planning to leave New Year's Day. The holidays that year were just long days to get through until we would be on our way. I hardly took time to think about Christmas — I was just anxious to get on with our new life.

The time flew by and soon it was time to rent a U-Haul for Todd's stuff. We would drive in the van and pull the trailer to California. I would be able to stay with him until time for me to begin my training in L.A., and I would still be able to go down on the weekends until I was sure he was ready for his new life. We were all set.

California, here we come!

When New Year's Eve came, Stacy and Todd wanted to go to Dallas to celebrate. It was the wee hours of the morning before the kids got back home and Todd was not feeling well. *Too much partying,* I thought.

I put Todd to bed about five o'clock New Year's Day, trying not to be angry with him. We needed to leave that day so my timing would work out to get him there and then start my new job. I had to be in Los Angeles, ready for my training, in one week.

Todd woke up later with chills and fever. Usually, that meant a bladder problem, so the doctor sent out some medication, but Todd only got worse.

Of course, we could not leave on New Year's Day. Monday came and he was no better. Tuesday, I called an ambulance to take him to the emergency room in Terrell. They took X-rays and discovered a gallstone the size of an egg — gallstones and bladder problems are common for quadriplegics, so I shouldn't have been surprised, but everything had been going so well!

My job, our move, everything had seemed ordained by the Lord. The U-Haul was packed and sitting in the driveway, Todd's new home was waiting and now this. Well, it couldn't be helped.

The doctors shattered Todd's gallstone with lasers and he then had to drink lots of liquids to rid his body of the pieces. Todd was in the hospital a week before I could bring him home.

It was time for me to go on to California for training. The kids and I were still in agreement that the job was too good to pass up. However, Todd's move to California was put on hold for awhile.

Todd...

I hired an aide, and made arrangements to have a nurse check on Todd while I was gone, then I flew to Los Angeles for my training. The training took five weeks, and I loved every minute of it. I called Todd every day and he was getting better, but his sickness had made him think twice about wanting to be on his own. He realized he could get sick anytime and he really needed someone he could count on to be there for him. He was reconsidering his move to California. I think for the first time, he felt vulnerable.

After my five week training period, there was a seminar in Dallas I had to attend, so I flew there along with my trainers and my new boss, Darlene. In Dallas, I was nearer Stacy and Todd, but it was still another week before I would be able to see them. It had been six weeks since I left.

It was February when we got to Dallas. A bit unusual for Texas, the weather had turned nasty. Snow was falling, and ice covered the streets, making for hazardous driving. Slipping and sliding back to our hotel from one of the night sessions, I was shocked speechless when who should be waiting for me in the lobby of the hotel but Todd and his friend Shaun. They had driven over from Emory that night in the snow and on the icy roads. But Todd had been anxious to see me. Since his accident, we had not been separated except for a day or two at a time and the week I was in the hospital with my back injury — the time we'd been apart had been hard on both of us.

"Todd, what are you doing here in this weather?" I scolded.

He came up with the lame excuse that they brought my coat to me. It was done now. There was no use fussing about it and I really was glad to see them. Also they were able to meet Darlene. The boys were awestruck with this gorgeous blonde, brown-eyed woman from California. Darlene and Todd hit it off right away.

The roads were getting worse so I couldn't let the boys drive back to Emory that night. I made them stay in my room. I didn't have the lift to get Todd into bed so I reclined his wheelchair, surrounded him with pillows and he slept in it all night. The next morning I called room service and ordered their breakfast.

After we finished eating our breakfast, Darlene came by to tell the boys goodbye, and I sent them back to Emory — not realizing the roads were even worse than the night before.

It took me over three hours to make the usual thirty minute trip to the airport to get the girls off on a plane back to California. I worried because I had sent the boys out on roads like that. Todd called me when they arrived home. It had taken them five hours to drive what should have been an hour and a half trip — I had to wait three more days before I could get home.

That week launched me on a new career that would send me traveling five states. I arranged my schedule so that I could still be home three nights a week. An aide stayed with Todd and the boys when I was gone, but I still wanted to do some of his personal care. I had always wanted someone else to physically take care of Todd so I could just be his mother, but now that I had the money to do it and Todd was willing, I found that my commitment to take care of him was as strong as ever.

When I traveled, I continued to call Todd every day to make sure he was okay and to make sure he was where he was supposed to be. I worried about things that could happen to him. I remembered the times he would ride off in his chair and we'd find him later down by the pond watching the ducks, or maybe we'd find him down in the edge of the woods watching the birds and the squirrels. There were times when my worry was well founded. Like the time when I missed Todd and started a search for him that led us down toward the woods. We saw him in the distance, his chair tilted to the side, one of the wheels stuck in a gopher hole. He was patiently waiting, humming to himself. He knew we'd find him sooner or later.

My first trip in my new job was to New Orleans. For three weeks I worked there, flying home on weekends. Like a bird out of a cage, I took in the city, trying wings that had been clipped for so long. My time was my own, and I was in charge of no one but me. It felt so good. Of course I was calling Todd every day, but I always heard,

"Everything's fine, Mom."

Todd was glad I was working and he was content to stay home. He had completely given up the idea of moving to California since his scare with the bladder infection.

My job was working out perfectly. I travelled a lot but I was also able to be home several days a week. I felt I had the best of both worlds. Eddie and I were still seeing each other but we both realized it would not be a permanent thing. He was a good man, and he was great with Todd, but I was looking for the man of my dreams and I hadn't met him yet.

When I was young, Clyde was my knight in shining armor and John Wayne rolled up in one. He had been the man of my dreams but he wasn't that man anymore — if he ever had been. I wasn't sure if there would ever be a special man in my life again, but I set about trying to find out.

Each year, Merle Norman Cosmetics held a convention. That spring, Dallas was the host city. One hundred Merle Norman staff members from the home office in Los Angeles attended. It was a great opportunity for me to meet many of them. Todd and Stacy went into Dallas with me and after the sessions, they would join me, Darlene and Laurie — the girls Todd met during the great ice storm. Darlene, Laurie, Todd and Stacy became fast friends as we toured Dallas and had fun together. It was exciting for me to see my children involved in what I was doing.

Stacy's graduation from high school was coming up. She had managed to get through her senior year but it had been rather ho-hum for her. It seemed she was always getting left overs since Todd's accident, and her graduation did not cause the stir that Todd's had. But she did get her diploma. She also agreed to take care of Todd for a year while I travelled with my job. It was a decision not made lightly, and it would help all three of us.

I planned to enroll Todd in college the next year. I had been planting the idea of college in Todd's mind for a long time and finally he seemed to be getting interested. He sent for information on different colleges and the two that seemed most promising for someone in his situation were the University of Texas at Arlington and Stephen F. Austin in Nacadoches, Texas.

Twice that year, Todd had to be hospitalized, but all in all, he seemed to be settling down and growing up. He had relationships with women and each time one seemed serious, the mother's heart in me would start dreaming about the day he would be able to marry and have a family. I knew if he could just get a college education, he would be able to have a position that would support a family. He couldn't comb his own hair, or shave himself, but I believed with all my heart that he would someday have his own home.

We checked out the University of Texas first, because Todd knew several kids who went there. We had a good time that day, but when I saw how handicap-oriented the campus was, I became very depressed. Even the man who took Todd's application was in a wheelchair. I suppose I was just being unrealistic. The idea was for Todd to be able to make it in college, but I wanted him to be in a normal environment. Todd liked the college in Arlington, but I just wasn't ready to give up yet. I made up my mind that I would visit the school in Nacadoches when I travelled the southern part of my territory with Merle Norman.

When I drove through the campus at Nacadoches, it felt like home, like the piney woods of East Texas where I was raised, and where Todd and Stacy were born. I hoped Todd would feel the same, and even though he had already made up his mind to go to Arlington, he fell in love with the place when we took a trip for him to check it out. There were wheelchair accessible apartments that were perfect for him, and when he found out the girls dormitory had a ramp, too, he was convinced. We were disappointed, because it was already too late for Todd to enroll for the fall semester so we would have to wait for spring. Stacy agreed to help us out until then, then she would be free to get on with her own life.

We decided this would be a good time to take a trip together as a family, so we made plans to visit a little town in Missouri I had been hearing a lot about called Branson. We loved country music, and Branson was said to have the best. Todd, Stacy, Brandon, and Eddie and his son Eric met me in Tulsa, Oklahoma, where I was working that week.

In Tulsa, I had arranged a surprise birthday party for Eddie with champagne and a big cake. He had done so much for my family, I wanted to do something special for him.

During the night, Todd got very sick, his temperature rising like it did when he had bladder problems. But after a good night's sleep he felt much better and wanted to go on to Branson. I got him up and dressed, then we headed toward Missouri. The trip was beautiful, the scenery breathtaking, but I was not prepared for all the traffic, the cars were bumper-to-bumper.

Dottie West was performing at Lowe's Theater, and I really wanted to see her because I had met her once when Clyde and I were first married.

TODD...

Her bus pulled up as I sat in the car waiting for Eddie to get our tickets. Star struck, I got out and hurried over to the bus, hoping to get a close look at her. Some guys in her band asked if they could help me, and I explained to them about Todd, and asked if he might be able meet Dottie. Tony, one of the guys, told me to meet him after the show and he'd see what he could do. I felt drawn to this guy for some reason and was thrilled, but when I got back to the car, Eddie was not too thrilled about me keeping him waiting while I talked to another man.

WE MET DOTTIE WEST IN BRANSON AND SHE SANG A SONG JUST TO TODD.
WHAT A WONDERFUL MEMORY FOR ALL OF US!

When the curtain came up my heart did a little flip flop. Tony was seated at the piano on stage. I was shocked — I thought he was just one of her stage hands, but it turned out that he was someone Dottie was actually promoting. He eventually became a star in Nashville thanks to her.

Tony had told me that his mom was in the audience and I was sure she was the lady sitting directly in front of Eddie and me. I tapped her on the shoulder.

"You're Tony's mom, aren't you?"

She turned to look at me and we were flabbergasted when we realized we knew each other — we had met soon after Todd's accident. Tony's mother and I renewed our acquaintance over dinner that night after the show. Then Tony invited us to go to their matinee the next day.

I was very excited, but Todd wasn't — he and the boys were more interested in girls than taking in a show. During the afternoon performance, he changed his mind.

"I'm glad to see Todd Odom here, all the way from Texas."

Todd's face flushed with pleasure as Dottie West acknowledged him from the stage. Tony had made sure Todd was down front in the theater, and during the show, Dottie came into the audience and sang a song directly to him. He became a fan of Dottie West that day, and it was mutual. Dottie took me aside later.

"I've fallen in love with that son of yours," she said. "Now you take good care of him, you hear?" *[Much later in my life, I found out that Dottie's drummer, who she had been in love with, had had an accident and been paralyzed like Todd. Todd reminded her of this man she loved.]*

We left Branson, going separate ways, me going toward my Arkansas assignment, and the others heading toward Texas, (Todd, with Dottie West's home phone number in his pocket). Each of us carried with us special memories of Branson, Missouri, a little town that has never quite let go of me.

In order to go to college, Todd needed an evaluation from Dallas Rehab to see if he was physically able. Before he did that, I had work to do on the road — and I also planned a fun time for Stacy and me.

Stacy flew to Memphis to meet me on the road and she and my niece, Tami and I spent a week there. The girls were on their own during the day while I worked, then we would go sightseeing together in the evenings. (We especially enjoyed visiting Graceland, home of Elvis Presley.)

As the week ended, Stacy and I headed back to Texas by way of Branson. When we got back into town, to our surprise we found that Dottie West was back at the Lowe's Theater. We went to see her show which turned out to be a birthday celebration for her. Dottie remembered us and asked all about Todd. I talked to Tony again, and thanked him for everything he had done for Todd.

As Stacy and I were leaving Branson, I just kept thinking, *There is something special here, some kind of peace I can't describe. I know I'm coming back here — I just don't know when.* Every time I had been to Branson, I had felt at home there — like my life was somehow connected to this small town. And, now I couldn't wait to go back, because of that wonderful sense of peace I always felt there.

My divorce became final the next week. It was sad that my marriage of more than twenty-seven years could be over in a few minutes. That was something I thought would never happen to Clyde and me, but I breathed a sigh of relief as I left the court room. I was glad it was over. Maybe now I could get on with my life.

Clyde and I had separated in July 1985, about two months after Todd's accident. We briefly got back together after Clyde's aneurysm, but separated for the last time in July 1986. I was not in a hurry to get a divorce because we needed his financial help — and I loved him and wanted our marriage to work. But, when I started going out in Todd's Junior year of high school, Clyde found out and *he asked me* for a divorce. *(Funny how quickly he reacted when the shoe was on the other foot!)* The whole process of getting a divorce drug on until October 31, 1989 when it was finally over. At the end, it was actually very peaceful in contrast to what our marriage had been. I just knew that Clyde would show up in court and fight, but he didn't. So, now I was on my own — really for the first time in my life.

CHAPTER 25
CODE RED

It was time for Todd to go to Dallas Rehab for tests that would determine if he was physically capable of going to college. I was confident that the tests would just be routine, but Todd dreaded everything.

I worked the Dallas area that week so I could see Todd every night and keep track of what was going on. I told the doctors that Todd had had some problems and I wanted to be very sure he would be in good shape physically to handle college.

The first good news I heard was that there had been some return of movement in an arm muscle. The doctors were sure that, with an operation, Todd could have use of one of his wrists. That meant he could feed himself and possibly even drive.

My joy at Todd regaining some arm movement was quickly over-shadowed by another test which showed that Todd had a severe kidney problem. Stones had shut down the function of one of his kidneys entirely. Lithotripsy would have to be performed.

Todd was moved from Dallas Rehab to Medical City where this simple procedure (lithotripsy) of crushing the stones would be done. After three hours, a doctor finally came out and told us they were not having much success. It had been necessary to put a stint — a tube — directly into the kidney to see if they could get it functioning again. If that didn't work, they would have to remove Todd's kidney.

Dallas Rehab put Todd's tests on hold and he was sent home until they could determine the outcome of the kidney.

Tubes were nothing new to us, but this time the tube was sticking out of his back, making it very difficult to dress him. His body jacket had to be put on just right or it would close the tube off. It was very frustrating.

Todd...

Trying to keep up with my job and also keep an eye on my son, I rearranged my schedule so that I would work close to home. We settled back into a routine. The hour-and-a-half each morning that I got him up was the time when Todd and I could talk freely. We shared many tears and a lot of laughter as we struggled with the very equipment that made it possible for him to lead an active life.

It was December of 1989 — four-and-a-half years since Todd's accident. The kidney finally kicked in and began to function normally. Once more he was poked and prodded by doctors who were confident this time the lithotripsy would work. They assured us the procedure would be relatively simple, but neither Todd nor I was totally convinced — it always seemed when doctors started telling us something would be simple, it usually wasn't. However, this time they were right. Todd came through the procedure with no problem, and the next morning they sent him home feeling great.

Soon after the lithotripsy, I had to fly to Los Angeles for more job training. Mamaw came to stay with him while I was gone. Stacy and the boys were there and a nurse would also be checking on him, so I felt he would be taken care of — besides, he assured me he was feeling fine.

I enjoyed the week I was in California with my Merle Norman family. They were good to me and very sympathetic about my family situation. I felt that things were once again on track, with my job and my family.

When I arrived home from California, Todd met me with his big grin as usual, glad to have me back. He looked so good. It was not until hours later that the boys told me Todd had not been feeling well. I figured it was just because he had the problem with his kidneys and dismissed it from my mind.

It was Saturday and Eddie and I went out for dinner that night leaving the boys. When we came in a few hours later, they were playing cards and dominoes.

Todd loved to play (even though someone had to make his plays for him) and didn't want to go to bed. I was irritated with him, but finally I gave up and went to bed — only to be awakened at five a.m. when he finally decided to go to bed. He was feeling good after his all night card playing spree.

Christmas holidays were approaching. Every year my dad had an early Christmas party with all his children, step-children, and grandchildren. Todd had only been in bed a couple of hours because of his all-night card and domino playing, but he insisted I get him up to go to my daddy's. I thought it would be better for him to stay home and rest after his sleepless night.

"I want to go to Grandpa Rufus' Christmas party too." He pouted, so against my better judgement, I got him ready.

The party was fun, as usual, with lots of food and everyone joining in to play games. Todd especially loved playing the games, but we had been there only a couple of hours when he said he wanted to go home.

"Todd, I tried to tell you to stay home and rest and now you want to go home," I grumbled.

"But I don't feel good, Mama." He looked very pale. We said goodbye to everyone and Stacy and I loaded him into the van and headed home. I had reclined Todd's chair in the back, but the hour and half trip was uncomfortable for him. He was feeling much worse, and I kept thinking, *If you had just not stayed up so late last night you wouldn't be sick.*

The trip seemed endless. We reached home a little after dark and I began my nightly ritual with him and did the transfer to bed.

"Mama," Todd said. "Will you sleep in here with me?"

I tucked the cover tightly around him to stop the chills that were shaking his body.

"Let me get my clothes changed and I'll be right back, okay?"

As I left the room, I still was not really concerned because this had happened so many times before. But soon, I began to sense there was something a little different this time.

"Mama, I just can't get warm," Todd said when I came back in the room. "Will you get me another blanket?"

He seemed a little scared, but I assured him this would pass like the other times.

All night, Todd's body shook with the chills that wouldn't let go. He did not want me to call the doctor, but after a sleepless night for both of us, I called him anyway. I explained that Todd's temperature had gone up to 105° during the night but came down with medication.

The doctor told me to bring him in and he would check him over. Todd and I remembered the many times we had been through similar situations since his accident and he always managed to be all right — it had almost become a routine. We knew he would be okay this time, too. But I was feeling something really strange, something about this time just didn't feel right.

We got Todd out of bed, and as I started to shampoo his hair, his face turned white.

"Mama, take me back to bed! I can't sit up. I'm gonna faint."

We couldn't get him in bed fast enough, he kept blacking out on us. I knew there was no other way to get him to the hospital except to call an ambulance. After I had called them, I began getting Todd's things together and even threw some things in a bag for me. Somehow, I just felt we would not be coming right back home.

When Todd first had his accident, we had become so use to Todd coming and going in ambulances, that it almost seemed routine — there is only so much stress that a mind can take. That morning, probably in some sort of denial, I had spent a considerable amount of time trying to coax a stray kitten to trust me and eat some food. Finally, I succeeded just before the ambulance came.

Stacy was still sleeping, so she didn't even know there was anything going on. I went into her room and touched her shoulder.

"Stacy, there's an ambulance here to pick Todd up," I said matter-of-factly. "We're going to the emergency room. I'll call you later and give you a report. Oh, yes, I found this little kitten in the garage." I put the yellow ball of fur beside her. "This little kitty'll take care of you while I'm gone."

Many times during the last four-and-a-half years, an ambulance had come to take Todd away, but there was something different this time. Todd was apprehensive, so I rode in the ambulance beside him as we made the hour-and-a-half trip to Dallas.

When we arrived at the hospital, Todd was rushed into the emergency room, but the doctors couldn't find what his problem was. His temperature kept climbing, and he asked me to hold his head. So once more I held a wet cloth on my son's forehead. It seemed just like when all this began so many years before.

Tests were run, then X-rays. Finally, after what seemed an eternity, Todd was admitted into the hospital.

"Mama, will you pray for me?" he asked when he was settled.

I stood by his bed and reached out to touch him.

"Oh Lord, touch us this hour," I prayed. "We need to feel your Spirit upon us. Heal Todd and give him strength to endure this, and give me peace that I might know what to say and do. Hold us in *Your Presence*. Amen."

My prayer seemed to comfort Todd, but I was afraid God didn't really hear me. I felt I had once again gotten so busy that my spiritual life was suffering. *Oh God, hear my prayer!*

Todd was restless and he seemed very anxious. We had only been in the room about an hour.

"Mama, get me an Ambu bag. I can't breathe!"

I hurried to the nurses' station, but they wouldn't let me have one without a doctor's order. I ran down the hall to the room and explained to Todd that the nurse could not release one without a doctor's order.

"Mama, get me something," he begged. "I can't get my breath!" Todd was panic stricken.

I ran back to the nurses' station.

"Todd's got to have an Ambu bag. He can't breathe." Now I was beginning to panic. "I've been trained to use the bag, so please give me one. I'll take the responsibility. I'll sign whatever you want — just give me the Ambu bag! Now!"

One of the nurses realized something really must be wrong and quickly unlocked their supply room and handed me an Ambu bag. I tried to force air into Todd's lungs, but it wasn't enough.

A nurse came rushing in and immediately began taking Todd's blood pressure. I could tell by her face it was going crazy. She got on the speaker to the nurses station and said, "This is a red code. This is a red code!"

They brought oxygen in and put the little tube around his head and inserted it at the base of his nose — it still wasn't enough. The doctor called and said to take him to the coronary unit. His blood pressure was so high they were afraid his heart would explode.

The staff were so busy working on Todd, they didn't even have time to notice that I was still in the room with them. As they left the room with his bed, I latched on like glue, I wasn't about to let them leave me behind. They rushed onto the waiting elevator that took us to the coronary care unit. I watched as they wheeled him to one of the tiny cubicles, working with him all the way. They started putting tubes everywhere and gave him medication trying to bring him around.

He was dying. I knew he was dying.

The doctors didn't make me leave the coronary care unit. I sat beside Todd the rest of the night, constantly keeping the wet cloth to his head, wiping his face, remembering so many other times when God brought him through, praying that He would fix it this time, too. Morning finally came, and Todd was not better. I was so tired — I had been standing by his bed all night.

"Todd," I said. "Mama is so tired. If I'll only be gone a little while, can I go lie down, just for a few minutes?"

He was so sweet as he said,

"I know you're tired, Mama, but don't be gone very long, okay?" Todd was so sweet and so very brave.

Oh, Lord, I thought. *Just let me lie down for just a minute.*

I walked out of the unit and down to the lobby. I laid my head down on the arm of a chair, but couldn't rest — I had to go back to Todd.

The head nurse had someone bring a chair to put beside Todd's bed for me — the doctors still had not pinpointed his problem.

Karen, Todd's former therapist from Dallas, and Sue, who was over the pulmonary department at Dallas Rehab, were both lung experts. When they heard that Todd had been brought in, they came and kept watch over Todd with me. I was concerned about his breathing. I knew Sue would keep a close eye on Todd because of what had happened at Baylor where Todd had been having seizures and had literally died before he was resuscitated and then transferred to St. Paul and on to Dallas Rehab. So, I was grateful for their concern, especially the next morning, when Todd's doctor called me into his office.

"Mrs. Odom, I want to know that Todd is dying," Dr. Shulkin said. "I don't know how he's made it through the night. He's a real fighter. But there's not any way, with the odds he has against him, that he can make it. We're still doing everything we can to keep him alive, but I don't know —"

"I know that you are," I said as his voice trailed off. "I watched through the night as your staff fought for him. I just don't understand why. Why now? Why now?"

I walked back out into the hallway overwhelmed and with tears streaming down my face. Feeling so helpless, I kept asking, *Why, God? Why now, just when he's getting his life together? He's planning to go to college soon, then he's supposed to meet a special girl and get married and have a family. Todd is supposed to outlive me — I'm the mama. How can he go first?*

I wandered around until I found the chapel and went inside. I fell to my knees. Weeping in helpless frustration, I cried out to God.

"I can't deal with this. We've come such a long way, why now? Why now? For over four years we've gone through things I just don't understand, and now this. Todd seemed to have everything going for him, and now I don't understand. Why?

"Lord," I said, raising my hands toward heaven. "I don't want to lose him! I don't want to lose him! I know we're never promised a lifetime with our children, but I'm not ready to let go. But, he's yours Lord and if you choose to take him, you're going to have to be there for me — because I can't do this by myself."

I sat there crying and crying, until, finally, I began to feel a real peace. I knew God heard my cry and that no matter what happened, he would be there to keep me lifted up.

Feeling much better, I went back to Todd. When Todd asked me to pray for him again, I knew this time God heard me. In the chapel, I had once more found the strength I needed, and through my prayer for him, Todd received a measure of peace, but he was still afraid.

God seemed to be lifting me above the shadows that were trying to envelope my son, and I was able to watch without tears as he struggled with what he knew was death. Fighting constantly for breath, Todd became very agitated and angry, experiencing the same thing he had gone through at Baylor, soon after the accident.

I explained to Dr. Shulkin the reason for his behavior, why he was fighting the oxygen mask and talking out of his head, and how they finally helped him at Baylor by putting an airway into his lungs. Unconvinced, Dr. Shulkin ordered one more test, but when it proved nothing, he came back into the room, and looked at me.

"Let's do it. Let's put the airway down."

"Thank you," I sighed with relief.

I knew that once the airway was in and Todd could breathe, everything would be alright — just as it had been at Baylor when the same thing happened. My excitement turned to horror when I found out that in order to put the tube in Todd's throat and into his lungs, they'd had to give him medicine that paralyzed him completely — leaving no movement at all. None!

After the procedure, I had to force my tears back and hold on to my last reserve of strength. I couldn't break down in front of Todd.

I will never forget the look Todd gave me. Unable to talk or turn his head, he managed to get his anger and disappointment across to me through those green eyes. He couldn't believe I would let them do this to him. All I could do was hold him and pray, trying to make him believe everything would be all right.

Stacy joined me at the hospital on Wednesday. She was very quiet, except when she was with Todd, but he seemed unaware she was there.

Todd was slipping away from us. He had begun to swell and his skin turned yellow. Dr. Shulkin told us he had gone into toxic shock. Poisonous fluids had taken over his body. They had moved Todd into a new kind of bed this time, one filled with warm sand, that shifted continuously — it was so much better than the rotating one. It also weighed him every hour. In less than forty-eight hours, Todd had gained sixty-five pounds of toxic fluid.

I needed my pastor, I needed him to pray with me so I asked a friend to tell him what was going on. Brother Jeff came immediately, and even though his wife was expecting a baby any day, he stayed at the hospital with us constantly. I've come to think God delayed the baby's birth so Brother

Jeff would have time to be with us, to pray and give us the counselling we needed. The presence of the Lord was there and a great peace.

Because Todd loved music so much, I brought gospel music tapes into his room. And I knew that, somehow, even in his delirium, he was hearing, *"Don't give up on the Brink of a Miracle."* I played it over and over again. If only those green eyes would open, I knew they would talk to me.

In the long days that passed, I prayed over Todd. I'd lean close to his ear and begin praying and talking to him, with the hope he could hear me, but he seemed to be slipping further and further away from us.

Dr. Shulkin took me aside on Friday and told me that the medication they had to give Todd to save his life was concentrating the blood supply to all his main organs leaving his limbs without blood supply. If he lived, he would probably lose his limbs. The very medication that was keeping Todd alive would cause his arms and legs to die. Todd had already lost so much, now this? I held on to the Lord, knowing he was the only one who could help us bear this frightening new development. Summoning strength from God, I straightened my shoulders.

"You know doctor," I quipped. "I've always had such a hard time getting Todd's jeans long enough — if we have to do this, we have to do it. Then I can buy him any length jeans I want," I smiled at the doctor. "And it's always been a hassle to get his cowboy boots on him, now I can just set them on his foot peddles. The best part is that he's still alive!"

Dr. Shulkin managed a tight smile, and I saw the tension relax a little in his face.

We had all dreamed of the day Todd would walk, but his life was tremendously more important than arms and legs he couldn't use anyway. We would still have the joy of having *him*.

It had only been five days since we brought Todd to the hospital but it seemed an eternity. Christmas was around the corner but there would be no shopping this year. Christmas Eve was on Saturday, and I did have something for Todd and Stacy... I had remembered Todd wanted a watch for Christmas, on my way back from Los Angeles I had picked up one and even wrapped it for him.

And somewhere along the way, I had bought a toy pig for Stacy from a Merle Norman Studio. It was a pink furry pig that walked and said, "Oink! Oink!" I had gift wrapped it also. It was a silly thing, but it would have to do for now.

On Christmas Eve Todd's eyelids began to flutter a little. He was trying to wake up. He was trying to come back to us. Finally, he began to focus and communicate with his eyes. He couldn't talk because of the airway, but Todd was back. He wanted me to pray for him, so I prayed for God's guidance and that he would keep Todd from being afraid. We could feel his presence. Tears were streaming down Todd's face, and I wondered what he was thinking as he lay there on Christmas Eve. The doctors were amazed that he was still hanging on, but I could not imagine Todd dying. He was too strong and he was a fighter. He was also too stubborn and he wanted to live.

Stacy came back that night. She had been with the family because it was Christmas. I didn't go anywhere. My Christmas that year was Todd. He had started his journey back to us and I couldn't leave him. I watched his monitor as he slipped in and out of the delirium. He had reached almost normal patterns on the monitor. His blood pressure was very low but his heart rhythm was pretty normal. We were told to talk loud and act natural around Todd, so we acted as normal as we could, trying to help him stay with us.

We got my gifts for Stacy and Todd out of the car. I unwrapped Todd's watch and held it in front of his eyes, and the monitor showed his blood pressure rise a little. I knew he was aware that he got a watch for Christmas. Stacy opened her gift and brought the pig out. She turned it on and it began to oink. With a teasing smile, she held it to Todd's face as though it was kissing him. His blood pressure rose higher. We knew he was angry with Stacy for teasing him. He was going to be all right. I knew it. I just knew it!

Christmas Day was a happy time because we saw Todd regain some consciousness. Then my heart dropped later that evening as I noticed Todd's eyes fluttering as if they were trying to roll back in his head. *These are not seizures,* I insisted to myself. I asked the nurse on duty.

"I'm not seeing what I think I'm seeing, am I?"

"If it's slight seizures, yes," she said.

I didn't want that happening again like it did at Baylor. *But,* I thought. *He got through that and he can do it this time, too.*

The doctors did more tests, this time to see how much, if any, of Todd's brain was still functioning.

I felt hopeful. He had gone through so much, I knew he would make it. But, the doctors were not as positive as I would have liked them to be. They were surprised that Todd had fought through this far, and they painted a bleak picture.

"Todd is a fighter," they admitted. "And there is a small chance he can recover, but we just can't say."

But I saw it differently. They hadn't told me Todd's brain was no longer functioning. They hadn't told me Todd was dead. I took the report as reason to hope. My faith had become strong and I felt such power inside. God was with me, and I could feel his sweetness filling me. He never left my side. I felt joy instead of tears, and I could smile and share my faith with others at the hospital who were hurting. I was getting to really know God. He was real. This spiritual side of me was real. I was not just going through an emotional experience. He was real!

Stacy was always there for me, and her support was precious. I leaned on her constantly, but there was a power inside me I had never had before. I knew people thought it strange that I was able to smile and talk so positively during such a traumatic situation.

Then the doctors started saying, "We think Todd's going to live." But before our hopes leaped too high, they added, "But we can't be sure just what shape he'll be in."

With the seizures and the lost blood circulation, I knew Todd could be brain damaged, as well as lose his arms and legs.

I was introduced to the orthopedic doctors who would do the amputation surgery on Todd. They showed me exactly where they would take his legs off — his legs and feet had turned black. (When someone came in to visit Todd I always made sure his legs were covered.)

Todd had lost the poisonous fluids from his body so he was not swollen now. I kept him fixed up nice so he looked like his old self, but I was seeing him slip away from us again. He was less and less "there". I just ignored the signs and talked to him as I always did. I still let him hear his music tapes. Over and over I would play, *"Don't Give Up on the Brink of a Miracle."* The words carried such hope, and listening to that song could make me believe we really were on the brink of a miracle.

> *"Don't give up on the brink of a miracle*
> *God is watching you*
> *Don't give up on the brink of a miracle*
> *He'll see you through."*

Todd knew God was watching over him. We were living one moment at a time. I would not give up. Another EEG was scheduled but I wasn't worried — I knew Todd would live.

We had gone through the holidays with hardly a thought about the usual presents and parties. Christmas had brought with it its real meaning. I learned that Jesus is real and our only hope is in Him.

My job had been put on hold for the past two weeks, and I wondered what would happen there. Also Stacy needed to get back to a normal routine. I needed to make some decisions. Todd was now hooked up to a life support system and this could go on for months. It was time to have a talk with his doctor. I needed to say something while I still believed Todd would live.

I met Dr. Shulkin in the hallway and asked for a minute to talk with him. He had been such a great strength for me and was always ready to stop and talk.

"Doctor," I said. "While I've still got my senses about me, I want to say that at the point when you know Todd is gone, I want him off life support — he's been through enough. Please spare him that. Please spare us that."

Stacy's friends in Emory were having a get together New year's Eve and I insisted she go.

"We'll probably be here a long time — this could go on for months," I told her. "You need to go and get away for awhile. Just please be back early tomorrow evening, okay? I need you."

She left, promising to be back early.

CHAPTER 26
SAYING GOODBYE

New Year's Day was on Sunday and the hospital was quiet. I felt God gave me that day to be alone with Todd. It was not a lonely day. I sat by Todd's bed watching him. There was no special nurse that day, no one to bathe him or to look after him. I just watched him, knowing he was no longer there.

"He's gone," I said to the empty room, as I gently touched Todd's beautiful face. I got up out of my chair, went to the double doors in our little cubicle and gently closed them, then went back to the bed and laid my head on Todd's chest and cried... And cried... And cried... And cried. I just allowed myself to let go realizing we were near the end. I felt as if I were in a trance. I spent some time in the chapel, praying, it was peaceful and quiet in that little sanctuary.

Stacy got back around eight o'clock New Years night and I could hardly wait for her to get to the hospital. When she came I met her in the lobby but did not tell her what I felt. We just quietly walked into his room and stood beside his bed, silent. I saw Stacy begin to cry and I knew that she knew. There was nothing to do, nothing to say. We stood together and watched Todd and listened to machines going through their useless routine, then we left the room. We drove to Aunt Ruth's house, which was only five minutes from the hospital, and went to bed. I lay there awhile.

"Stacy," I said. "I'm going back. I want to go stay with Todd."

"Me too," she responded.

On the way back to the hospital we were able to share our feelings with each other. Before, we had talked only about Todd living and getting better, but now, we let him go. We talked of Heaven and how we knew Todd was with Jesus.

When we were once more in Todd's room, Stacy and I cried together. Since there was only a small staff during the holidays, they had allowed drool to slide down Todd's face and no one had bothered to wipe it away. His face was greasy and his hair was a mess — it was all coming out because of the medication. We gave way to tears for Todd and his years of painful helplessness, and for our own selves. We missed him.

In the wee hours of the morning Stacy and I went back to Aunt Ruth's and got some sleep. I awoke early, and without waking Stacy, I hurried back to the hospital. I felt better just being there, and I knew if Todd knew I was there, he would feel better, too.

I went into Todd's room and shut the door. The nurses, always very understanding, didn't say a word. I, once again, just laid my head on Todd's chest and cried. I did not cry out to God, I just freed all the pent up emotions inside. After I cried, I blew my nose, wiped my eyes and got up.

"You're going to get a bath, Todd," I said to him determinedly. "You're going to get cleaned up today — you have a journey to make."

I went to the nurses' station and asked someone to get me a pan of water.

"Todd needs a bath," I answered their questioning look. "He's also going to get a haircut." His hair had gotten so long and thin and ugly — it was time to get him looking good again. I drove back to Aunt Ruth's and picked up Stacy, and my scissors.

"Todd's going to get a haircut today," I said, and Stacy and I headed back to the hospital.

The nurses had already bathed Todd by the time we got there, so I put Todd's music on and cut and washed his hair. He looked beautiful, so peaceful, like he was only asleep.

Later, Stacy and I met another of Todd's doctors, Dr. Logan, in the hallway. With a serious frown on his face, he put out his hand for us to stop.

"We don't know how, but Todd seems to be surviving this."

They had just seen something on the EEG and felt Todd might live.

How can they tell me this, I thought. *I've just given him up.*

I didn't want false hope, or to have to go through again what I had just gone through.

The doctor walked back to the room with us and there were several people with Todd, all seeming to think he was better. Stacy and I walked to the area where Brother Jeff and some of our family and friends were waiting. When I told them what was going on, Brother Jeff wanted to go into Todd's room and pray for him. We all made a circle around Todd's bed, Stacy, Amy, Karen, Brother Jeff, another minister we had met at the hospital, and myself. As Brother Jeff began to pray it was as if the room was lifted up. I didn't understand it, but I knew the Holy Spirit was in that room — we could feel the presence of the Lord there. Since I was a little girl, in the Baptist Church in East Texas, I had believed I was a Christian, but I had never felt the Spirit of God like I did that day. I saw by the look on the other's faces that they felt the same.

"What did we just experience in there?" I asked Brother Jeff as we walked out of the room.

"I don't know, I can't explain it. I just know I have never experienced anything like that before." He disappeared while everyone else was trying to explain what had happened.

After Dr. Logan had told us that Todd may survive, we were held in suspension not knowing what to do next. I had been ready to tell the doctors to unhook Todd's ventilator, but now felt renewed hope. *Maybe. Just maybe.*

Brother Jeff came back to the waiting room after an hour or so.

"I just had to get away," he said. "I had to be alone with God for awhile." He held his Bible between us. "Terry, God gave me a scripture for you. 'Be still and know that I am God.'"

I am such a hyper person, God had to slow me down. That scripture made me remember something very important, God was in control. We were not surprised when the doctor came to us and said they were not ready to give up yet. They were not taking Todd off the support system.

"I can't go back to Aunt Ruth's tonight," I told Stacy. "I've got to have some quiet time."

My friend Eddie came to see Todd that evening, and after he left, Stacy and I went to the Holiday Inn for the night. I relaxed a little, then called my dad. We talked and talked. I shared my new found faith, and my hope, now, that Todd would live, and not only live, but I had never said this before, but...

"Daddy, I believe if Todd does live... If he lives, he will walk again."

That night I slept soundly and still felt hopeful when I returned to the hospital because of what had happened the day before. I felt I was being taken on a journey and was extremely happy.

The boys who were staying in our home came to see Todd that day, and also some of the girls Todd was crazy about. It was the first time they had seen him since he had gotten so bad, and it was very hard for them. They felt such a sense of loss, and these tough redneck guys cried as they talked to Todd.

"Todd you can't leave us. You can't die. You just can't die!"

The boys sobbed like little babies and my heart was full as I watched them. Then the girls came in and stood by Todd's bed, stroking his hair and talking to him as the tears streamed down their faces. I swore Todd's blood pressure went up and down. I became very excited because Todd knew his friends were there.

A few days later another EEG was done — no change.

"If anything," his doctor said. "It's a little worse."

I had to face the fact that if Todd lived, unless God did do a miracle, there was a good possibility there would be brain damage. I began seriously dealing with this in my mind.

When Todd had the accident and had become paralyzed, I had just gathered up myself and did what needed to be done. I had handled the situation. I had dealt with the spinal cord injury because I still had Todd. *I don't think I can handle brain damage,* I told the Lord. I was now face to face with one of my greatest fears. I remembered when we were staying at Ronald McDonald House and the brain damaged child I had seen there. I remembered telling Clyde that we could survive because at least Todd still had his mind. What if he didn't now?

Saturday, January sixth, no change. Sunday, the seventh, still the same. Another EEG was scheduled for Monday, the eighth. I knew Todd would live now, but I felt he would be brain damaged.

"Be still and know that I Am God," I repeated to myself the scripture Brother Jeff had given to me. "Be still and know that I am God." And then I knew: God had brought me through some hard places — and with that same mercy and grace, he would bring me through anything I faced in the future — even brain damage.

Monday, the eighth, another EEG was run. I tried to wake Todd up. In desperation, I yelled in his face, I shook him, I even pinched him, no response.

Brother Jeff walked into the room just as I hysterically slapped Todd's face. I screamed as Todd's eyes flung wide open. He was looking straight at me. The doctor hurried in the room.

"Please step outside," he said.

"He opened his eyes!" I gasped. "I saw him open his eyes."

Brother Jeff and I followed the doctor into the hall.

"It's much, much worse," he said. "We feel we should take him off the system."

"No! No! I just saw him open his eyes!" I cried out.

The doctor explained to me that Todd's opening his eyes was just a automatic reaction — that was all. Todd was no longer there.

"Not now. I can't give him up now," I pleaded with the doctor. "I don't understand." I was an emotional wreck. Hope seemed to be dangled in front of me one minute, then jerked away the next. It was a horrible joke.

"You've got time," the doctor said. "You don't have to decide today."

"I've got to go home," I told Brother Jeff. I knew I was close to hysterics. "I've got to get myself together. I can't deal with this now. I've had such faith — I've felt so strong. God, where are you? I can't take this." I felt so forsaken.

Brother Jeff and I walked to the chapel,. As I began to pray, I felt a calmness soothing my shattered nerves. I told Brother Jeff that I needed to go talk to Clyde.

"I can't do this by myself," I said.

Then I realized how unfair it was for me to try to make such a decision alone. I needed Todd's dad. I know, now, that God had not forsaken me, he simply wanted me to stop depending on myself and let Clyde help make the decision. In His wisdom, God saw the danger of me making such a decision by myself. There would be too much room for blame if I took it on myself to make this decision alone.

I called Clyde and told him we were coming to talk with him. Stacy did not want to talk to her daddy, so Brother Jeff, Karen from Texas Rehab, and I drove to Emory. Clyde's health still was not good, but I had talked to him every day, keeping him updated on Todd's condition.

Clyde and Sue, his newest girlfriend, were there when we got to his house. He seemed very much in control at first, but as we talked, he became more emotional. He agreed to go back with me to the hospital the next day. He wanted to sit down with the doctors so he could know for himself exactly how Todd's brain was doing. I couldn't tell how Clyde really felt, but I was glad he'd agreed to go back with me.

Clyde called the house the next morning where I had spent the night alone. He was glad no one was there with me because he could not hold back his tears as we talked.

"Terry, what do you think about Todd?" he asked, his voice thick with tears.

"I think Todd is gone, Clyde," I answered, calmly. "I think he was gone after the first of January, but I just couldn't make the decision to take him off life support by myself."

"Terry, I don't want to kill him," Clyde said.

"Kill him? Do you think that's what I want?" I was crying now, too. "When you were in the hospital, the doctors gave you a one percent chance of living with an operation and no chance of living without it. I chose the operation for you," I sobbed. "But let me ask you something, if you had it to do over which would you choose?"

"That makes it a little bit easier, because I would choose to die," Clyde said honestly. "I would never have wanted to live like I've lived the last few years."

"Then that tells us what we have to do for Todd," I said quietly. "We have to love him enough to let him go."

We agreed that prolonging the agony of his life would do him no good. Todd would not choose to be kept alive when there was no life. We sadly hung up the phone. I began that day making preparations to bring Todd home to Emory.

That afternoon, Clyde and Sue and I met with the doctors and heard them say Todd's brain had died, there were no brain waves.

"It's time to take him off the support," they said with pity for us.

"Please do one more EEG," Clyde pleaded.

He had not seen Todd at all during the past weeks so he didn't know the changes that had taken place. For him, to go in and see Todd was the most traumatic thing he had ever gone through.

Clyde was in a wheelchair, and we pushed him into Todd's room and closed the door. Clyde, his body shaking with grief, rose from the chair and stood by Todd's bed. He reached out to touch the son who had played football, the son in whom he'd had such hope.

"Oh, Lord, how do we get past this?" he cried.

In a little while, Clyde, still shaking, sat down in his chair, and we went back out into the hall. Clyde reluctantly agreed that Todd was gone, but wanted one more EEG. If there was no change, he should be taken off the support. Clyde and Sue left, promising to be back on Thursday, two days away.

During those two days, I spent a lot of time with Todd, just holding his hand and crying and letting myself grieve, knowing I had only a short time to physically be with him. Time was rushing by, and soon the family would be coming to say goodbye to Todd and there would be no more time for me to be alone with him.

Although I knew Todd was in Heaven with Jesus, and I didn't have to worry about him hurting anymore, in the midst of my grieving for him I suddenly felt very alone. I hurt so badly and felt completely isolated with my pain. But through my tears, I realized my faith was strong.

On Wednesday night I got a disturbing phone call from Todd's high school counselor.

"Terry, I just heard," she said. Her voice rose and she seemed on the edge of hysteria. "Don't let them take him off the ventilator. Don't you dare let them take him off!" She said that she and her husband were coming right then to the hospital to talk to me.

Delores, her husband and little girl came and insisted I leave the hospital with them. There were so many people around and so much confusion, I agreed to go to a restaurant with them. Delores had lost a son in a three wheeler accident during Todd's junior year in high school. They had been forced to take him off the ventilator, and she was beside herself thinking about the same thing happening to us. She begged me not to do it.

"Lord," I prayed. "Please get me out of this." I understood her pain, but I felt I was going to explode. I had just begun to feel we were doing the right thing, and now this!

Finally, they took me back to the hospital, but when I went in, none of my family was there. Where was Stacy? I needed her!

Someone told me that Stacy and her cousin Tami had gone to eat. I panicked. I ran up to the balcony that overlooked the main floor of the hospital where I paced and hugged a pillow waiting for them to return.

I saw them when they came through the door. Suddenly, overcome with joy at seeing them, I threw the pillow I was holding over the balcony railing at them and then ran down to the waiting room literally jumping into Stacy's lap.

"Don't ever leave me again!" I pleaded.

"See," Stacy said to Tami, with a teasing smile. "I told you she'd be like this when we got back."

Our laughter broke the night silence of the hospital and helped ease some of our sorrow. We spent the night with Todd, talking to him and each other — knowing this was the last night.

Thursday came too soon, but the day was peaceful. There was a peace over the whole hospital. A room had been reserved for our family for that morning. It was eight o'clock, and Stacy and I were alone in the family room. I felt this was the perfect time to share with her my feelings over the past three and a half weeks. So I took her hand and we sat on the couch.

"Stacy, I said. "I don't know what you've thought about me in the last weeks but my life is changed. I'm not the same person that I was when I brought Todd here. We always felt Todd was chosen for something special — that he was chosen of God to do something with his life. I know now, it wasn't only Todd that was chosen, it was me, too."

"Me, too, Mama," Stacy said.

We both began laughing because we knew that God had done a work in both of us during this time. He chose both of us — as well as you who are reading this. He chooses all of us, if we will.

The others who had been invited to be with Todd when we said goodbye started to arrive. Brother Jeff, Karen from Dallas Rehab, Laverne Morris, my dad and Edie my stepmom, Stacy's friend Amy, my niece Tami, and Clyde and Sue.

It was time to run the EEG. Waiting for the results, we filed in and out of Todd's room — each one saying his own goodbyes.

The results came — no change. The papers were signed. First mine, then Clyde's.

Brother Jeff went in with Todd to stay until it was over. I wanted to go but Clyde held me back.

"You don't need to be there, Terry." He wanted to spare me.

I wish I had insisted.

After a few minutes, Brother Jeff came out.

"They removed the ventilator and he never moved. He just kept sleeping gently in Jesus."

"Praise God!" I cried as I hugged the doctor. "He's free. He's in Heaven, and he's safe!"

Everyone went in one more time to see Todd — but this time it was truly wonderful. The tubes were gone. He looked beautiful. There was a smile on his face and he looked so peaceful. I laid across his chest for the last time and cried.

Stacy and Clyde were crying, too, but we all knew he was free, and we were very, very thankful.

We had made many friends in the hospital, so there were goodbyes and hugs to share, but we left the hospital bathed in a wonderful peace.

As we stepped off the elevator, I excused myself so I could make one more phone call.

"He's free, Darlene. Our Todd's free at last." My heart sang as I told my boss Darlene how much I loved her and how precious she had become to me and to Todd. She and Laurie would be at the funeral, she said.

Hanging up the phone, I went back to join Brother Jeff and Stacy. As I rounded the corner, I saw a man in a wheelchair — and my heart leaped for a moment because — just for one moment, I thought I was seeing Todd up and around in his chair — but, then my vision and reality refocused and I continued on down the hallway. Brother Jeff, Stacy and I went down in the elevator in complete silence, but as we got off and walked towards the front doors of the hospital, I linked arms with them and began to sing:

"I'll have a new body, praise the Lord. I'll have a new life..."

Brother Jeff and Stacy joined in and we left the hospital singing.

"Brother Jeff," I said, "I want that song sung at Todd's funeral."

"I don't believe I've ever heard that song at a funeral, Terry," Brother Jeff commented with a smile.

"Well, it's going to be sung at Todd's," I insisted. "Because he's got a new body and he's got a new life. He's out of his wheelchair now. Todd is free! My son is free!"

REMEMBERING

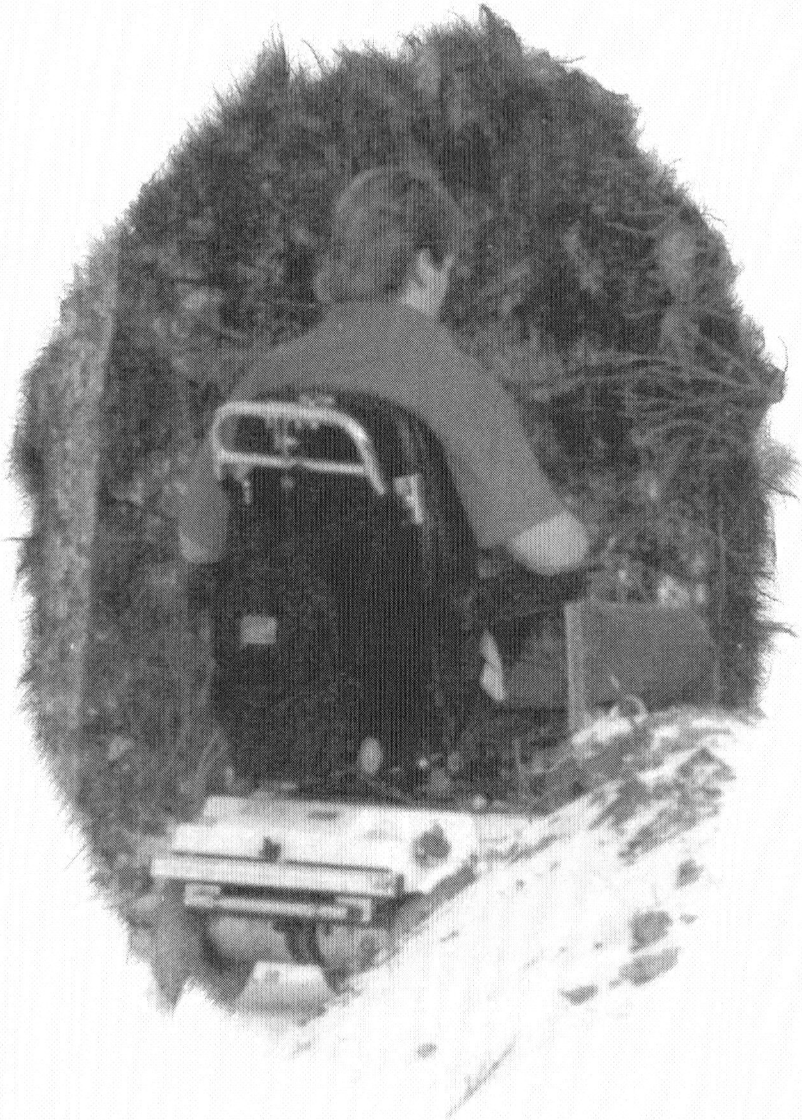

MY FRIEND, TODD

My friend, Todd, died today,
The Master decided to take him away;

Though heavy the burdens of sorrow and pain,
We must realize our loss is Todd's biggest gain.

For today Todd met his Savior face to face,
And was given his portion of God's perfect place.

No longer in the wheelchair will his feet be bound,
Todd walked again today when his soul left the ground.

> Past gates of pearl and on streets
> Of the finest gold he did joyously roam
> You see today Todd got his wish,
> From his hospital bed he went home.

> Though Todd has left us,
> His Spirit's message will always remain
> Accept Jesus Christ as your Savior
> And you too will one day walk again.

Since I know he's happy I can proudly say,
My friend Todd Edward Odom lives today.

— *Mark Morris*

[TODD AND TIMMY JENNINGS]

PHOTO ESSAY
TODD... MY SON

MY FRIEND,

I WALKED WITH YOU.

AND KNEW YOU FOR SUCH A SHORT TIME.

YOU MADE US LAUGH.

WE REMEMBER WITH FONDNESS,

AND WITH A KNOWLEDGE AND HOPE,

THAT SOMEDAY,

WE WILL SEE YOU

ONCE AGAIN.

ON MY WEDDING DAY — I THOUGHT OUR STORY WOULD BE PERFECT

TODD'S STORY, OF COURSE, STARTS WITH MY LOVE AFFAIR WITH HIS
FATHER CLYDE. I'D LOVED CLYDE FOR WHAT SEEMED ALL MY LIFE.

NO MATTER WHAT HAD HAPPENED IN OUR MARRIAGE, I WAS ALWAYS
WILLING TO BELIEVE ANYTHING CLYDE TOLD ME BECAUSE I WAS SO
MUCH IN LOVE WITH HIM.

IN OUR 24 YEARS OF MARRIAGE, WE SEPARATED MANY TIMES. THE LAST
SEPARATION WAS THE SUMMER OF 1986 AND IT WAS THREE MORE YEARS
BEFORE OUR DIVORCE WAS FINALIZED.

WE WEREN'T A GREAT PICTURE-TAKING FAMILY, BUT HERE ARE
SOME OF THE MEMORIES THAT WERE CAPTURED ON FILM.

THIS WAS TAKEN AT CHURCH VERY EARLY IN OUR MARRIAGE

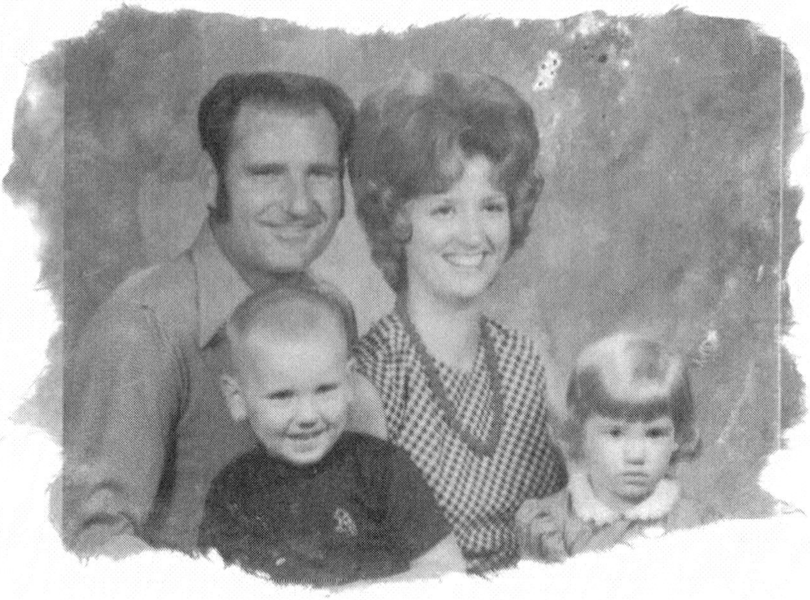

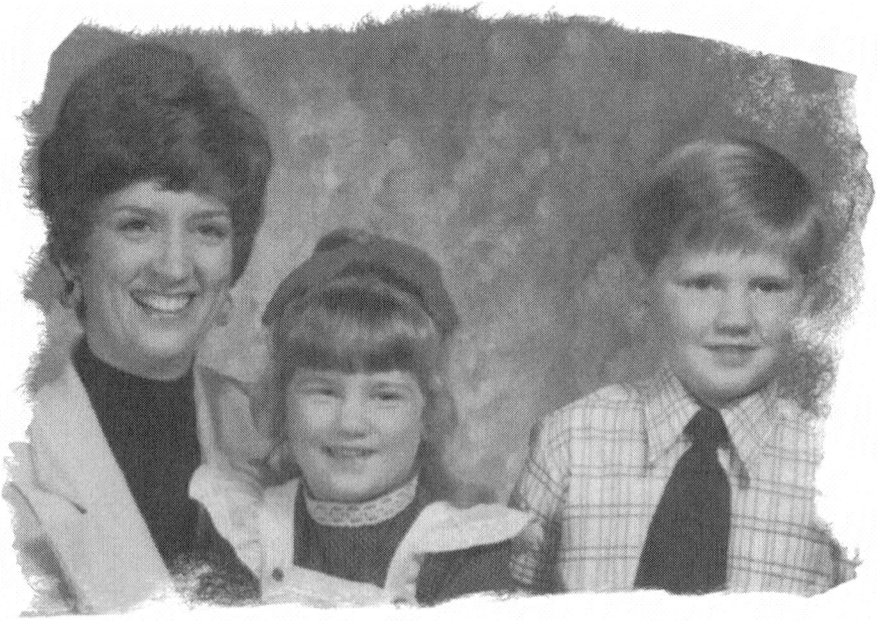

I ALWAYS THOUGHT OUR FAMILY LIFE WAS VERY GOOD —
BECAUSE MY HUSBAND LIVED TWO VERY SEPARATE LIVES AND
HE ALWAYS MADE ME FEEL VERY LOVED. BUT IT WAS INEVITABLE
THAT OUR MARRIAGE WOULD END IN DIVORCE WHEN I FINALLY
FOUND OUT ABOUT THE OTHER LIFE HE WAS LEADING.

THIS IS ONE OF MY FAVORITE PICTURES OF TODD
(FOR OBVIOUS SENTIMENTAL REASONS)

TODD 12 AND STACY 11 — I'M SO PROUD OF THEM!
THREE YEARS BEFORE THE ACCIDENT THAT CHANGED ALL OUR LIVES

LITTLE LEAGUE FOOTBALL 1979
TODD (NO. 21) AND CLYDE (BACK ROW MIDDLE)

LITTLE LEAGUE FOOTBALL 1980. TODD (NO. 75) AND TEAMMATES

BOTH TODD AND STACY HAD PARTICIPATED IN SPORTS SINCE THEY WERE ABOUT SIX YEARS OLD. BOTH PLAYED SOCCER, THEN STACY WENT ON TO VOLLEYBALL AND TODD TO FOOTBALL. AFTER TODD'S ACCIDENT AND I HAD TO BECOME SO INVOLVED WITH HIS CARE, STACY LOST INTEREST IN SPORTS BECAUSE WE WERE NO LONGER PARTICIPATING AS A FAMILY.

TODD'S EIGHTH GRADE GRADUATION — ONE YEAR LATER HIS DREAM TO BECOME A PROFESSIONAL FOOTBALL PLAYER WAS OVER

MY UNCLE COZELL (FAR LEFT) AND COUSINS TODD AND KEVIN

ON THE TARMAC IN THE BAHAMAS — TODD IS ALREADY TALLER THAN HIS FATHER, AND STACY IS DEFINITELY TALLER THAN ME

AT THE RODEO
TODD (FAR LEFT) AND CLYDE (SECOND FROM RIGHT) WITH FRIENDS
LESS THAN 2 MONTHS BEFORE HIS DIVING ACCIDENT

TODD IN IRON LUNG – JUST BEFORE HE WAS TAKEN OFF THE RESPIRATOR
(HE ONLY HAD TO SLEEP IN THE IRON LUNG AT NIGHT FOR A SHORT TIME
WHILE THEY WEANED HIM OFF THE RESPIRATOR)

THE COMMON AREA AT RONALD MCDONALD HOUSE — A WONDERFUL REFUGE
FOR US IN THE MIDST OF THE CHAOS SURROUNDING TODD'S ACCIDENT

TWO WEEKS AFTER TODD'S ACCIDENT, STACY HAD HER 14TH BIRTHDAY. WE WERE STAYING AT RONALD MCDONALD HOUSE, BUT WE STILL MANAGED TO HAVE A VERY NICE BIRTHDAY PARTY FOR HER.

STACY'S 14TH BIRTHDAY PARTY IN THE COMMON AREA AT RONALD MCDONALD HOUSE

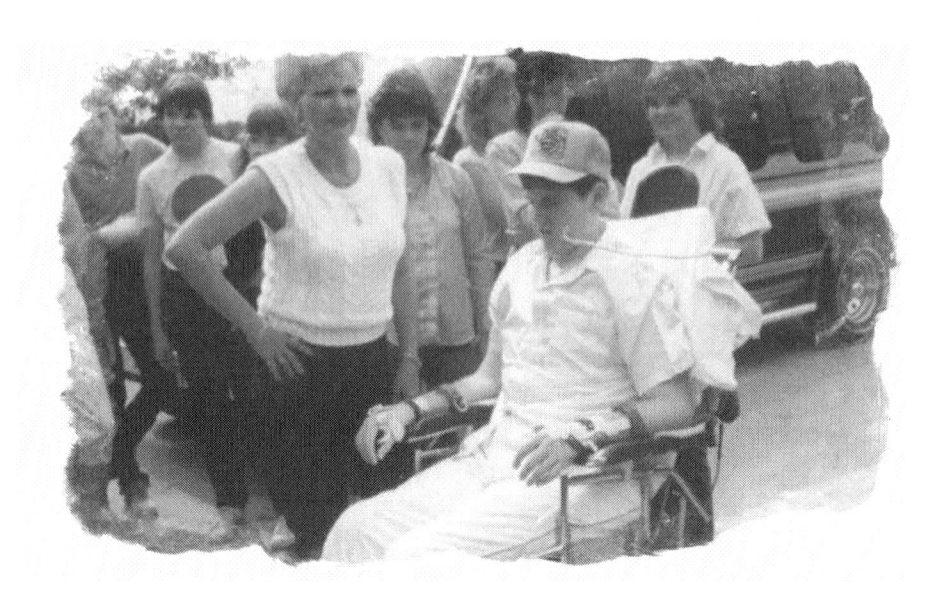

TODD'S HOMECOMING PARTY WITH HIS FRIENDS,
STILL 3 MONTHS TO GO BEFORE HE CAN COME HOME FOR GOOD!

THE SERIOUSNESS, THE FINALITY, THE PERMANENCY OF
TODD'S INJURY CAN BE SEE ON EVERYONE'S FACE

TODD WAS VERY SHY AT FIRST, THEN HE STARTED TO RELAX

EVERYONE WAS A LITTLE UNCOMFORTABLE AT FIRST,
BUT THEN THINGS STARTED TO LOOSEN UP

DON'T THINK WE DIDN'T HAVE FUN — TODD WAS VERY POPULAR AND WAS ALWAYS ON THE PHONE — AND THIS WAS STACY'S SOLUTION TO <u>NOT</u> HOLD THE PHONE SO SHE COULD DO WHAT SHE WANTED!

CLYDE HEARD THAT MONKEYS COULD BE TAUGHT TO FETCH THINGS FOR PARAPLEGICS — UNFORTUNATELY, THIS LITTLE MONKEY WOULDN'T AND BECAME STACY'S PET INSTEAD

WE MADE A PHOTO WALL FOR TODD SO THAT HE COULD SEE SOME FAMILIAR FRIENDS. ABOVE, BILLY BOB, HIS FAVORITE DOG. BELOW TODD AND STACY'S PET TIGER PICTURED WITH A NEIGHBOR BOY.

AS YOU CAN SEE, PETS WERE VERY IMPORTANT IN OUR HOUSE

TODD PLAYED FRESHMAN FOOTBALL FOR THE RAINES WILDCATS.
AT THE END OF HIS FRESHMAN YEAR AT RAINES HIGH SCHOOL, HE WAS
VOTED ON THE VARSITY TEAM BECAUSE OF HIS PLAYING ABILITY.
TODD ACTUALLY PLAYED 1 OR 2 GAMES AS A VARSITY FOOTBALL PLAYER FOR
THE WILDCATS DURING HIS FRESHMAN YEAR. ABOVE TODD IS PICTURED WITH
FOOTBALL PLAYER KINDLE (CIRCLED), A GRADUATING SENIOR.
TODD WAS TO TAKE HIS PLACE ON THE RAINES WILDCATS
VARSITY TEAM STARTING IN HIS SOPHOMORE YEAR.

IT WAS ALWAYS CLYDE'S DREAM AND THEN TODD'S DREAM, FOR TODD TO BECOME A PROFESSIONAL FOOTBALL PLAYER. WHEN THAT COULDN'T HAPPEN, ONE MAN MADE SURE THAT TODD WAS STILL A PART OF THE TEAM – COACH BUSCH. I CAN NEVER THANK HIM ENOUGH FOR EVERYTHING HE DID TO MAKE TODD FEEL A PART OF THE RAINES WILDCATS AND FOR HELPING HIM ACHIEVE SUCCESS DURING THE REST OF HIS HIGH SCHOOL YEARS.

PEP RALLY – THE VARSITY RAINES WILDCATS
WITH HONORARY CAPTAIN TODD ODOM (NO. 64 ON FAR RIGHT)

FRIENDS ARE FRIENDS FOREVER!

WHAT CAN YOU REALLY SAY ABOUT FRIENDS? THERE WERE THE FRIENDS THAT CAME AND STAYED AT OUR HOUSE AND HELPED WITH TODD'S CARE. I CALLED THEM "THE BOYS". THEIR HELP ENABLED ME TO GO BACK TO SCHOOL AND THEN BACK TO WORK. I LAUGH TO THINK OF ALL THE TIMES THAT TODD'S VAN PULLED UP IN TOWN AND A BUNCH OF KIDS HUNG OUT FOR THE PARTY THAT WOULD ENSUE.

LAVERNE MORRIS AND HER SONS MARK AND "LITTLE TODD" WERE SO VERY PRECIOUS TO ME. LAVERNE SUPPORTED ME EMOTIONALLY AS I WENT THROUGH THE VERY HARD DAYS OF TAKING CARE OF TODD AND THEN GOING THROUGH THE END OF MY MARRIAGE. WITHOUT HER HELP, TODD WOULD NEVER HAVE GRADUATED HIGH SCHOOL. I CAN NEVER THANK HER ENOUGH.

THERE WERE ALSO SO MANY OF TODD'S FRIENDS WHO STOPPED BY AND HELPED DURING THOSE INITIAL DAYS OF ADJUSTMENT AND THEY STAYED WITH HIM THROUGHOUT THE REMAINDER OF HIS LIFE. I TRULY CAN NEVER EXPRESS MY APPRECIATION ENOUGH FOR ALL OF THE PEOPLE WHO IMPACTED TODD'S LIFE — THERE ARE JUST A FEW PICTURED HERE AND THROUGHOUT OTHER PAGES OF THE BOOK. FOR THE MANY OTHERS, I WISH I COULD INCLUDE PICTURES OF YOU ALL, BUT SPACE AND MISSING PHOTOS WILL NOT ALLOW — EACH ONE OF YOU SHOULD KNOW THAT I HAVE NOT FORGOTTEN WHO YOU ARE — AND I THANK YOU FROM THE BOTTOM OF MY HEART FOR BEING PART OF TODD'S LIFE AND FOR BEING A PART OF MINE. I LOVE ALL OF YOU FOR THE LOVE AND FRIENDSHIP YOU GAVE MY SON, TODD.

ROGER

BRANDON

ROGER AND BRANDON WERE TWO OF THE BOYS WHO STAYED WITH US. THEIR HELP ALLOWED ME TO RETURN TO WORK. I LOVED THEM SO MUCH FOR ALL THE HELP THEY GAVE OUR FAMILY AND FOR JUST BEING THEMSELVES.

JIMBO GAVE US HOPE. HE WENT ON TO CALIFORNIA TO GET AN APARTMENT THAT TODD WAS SUPPOSED TO SHARE. UNFORTUNATELY, THOSE PLANS DID NOT MATERIALIZE.

TODD'S "TEAM" –
T=TODD (BOTTOM CENTER), E=ERIC, A=ANTHONY, M=MICHAEL

TODD AND MARK MORRIS SHARING A SUNDAE ON "SENIOR DAY"

TAMI TAYLOR (TODD'S COUSIN) AND
KIM TERRY

LATONNA LAIR (ONE OF
TODD'S FAVORITE FRIENDS)

AMY KYLE (ONE OF STACY'S FRIENDS) AND SAM EDWARDS (ONE OF TODD'S
BEST FRIENDS) — AMY AND SAM EVENTUALLY MARRIED EACH OTHER

TAMMY MILEY, ME AND STACY — BEFORE THEY
LEFT FOR "DRESS UP DAY" AT SCHOOL

TODD AND STACY (NOT SHOWN) WERE BOTH IN THE SAME
PLAY AT RAINES HIGH SCHOOL — TODD (SHOWN HERE)
PLAYED A COMPUTER GEEK (YES, THAT'S A WIG)

STACY — PROM 1988

STACY AT 16

STACY WAS 13 WHEN TODD HAD HIS ACCIDENT. SUDDENLY
SHE HAD TO GROW UP AND TAKE ON MANY RESPONSIBILITIES
THAT SOME ADULTS NEVER HAVE TO FACE.

A HARDSHIP LICENSE SO THAT SHE COULD DRIVE TODD TO SCHOOL.
SHOPPING FOR HER OWN SCHOOL CLOTHES. LEARNING TO LEAN ON
HERSELF EMOTIONALLY BECAUSE MUCH OF MY TIME WAS TIED UP WITH
TAKING CARE OF TODD AND THEN CLYDE. DEALING WITH THE DIVORCE OF
HER PARENTS, TODD'S ACCIDENT, THE UNAVAILABILITY OF ADULTS IN HER
LIFE, AND THE MANY PEOPLE THAT SUDDENLY FILLED UP OUR HOME.

BUT THROUGH ALL OF THIS, STACY BECAME A VERY STRONG AND STABLE
PERSON — IN SPITE OF ALL THAT SHE HAD TO GO THROUGH.
TODAY, SHE IS MY VERY BEST FRIEND.

TODD AND STACY — HIGH SCHOOL SUDDENLY BECAME
VERY DIFFICULT FOR BOTH OF THEM

TODD AND STACY — TOO MUCH PARTYING MADE LIFE DIFFICULT

STACY'S GRADUATION PICTURE — 1989

JUNIOR PROM — TONI QUIZAR AND TODD.
I HAD DREAMS THAT THEY WOULD SOMEDAY GET MARRIED.

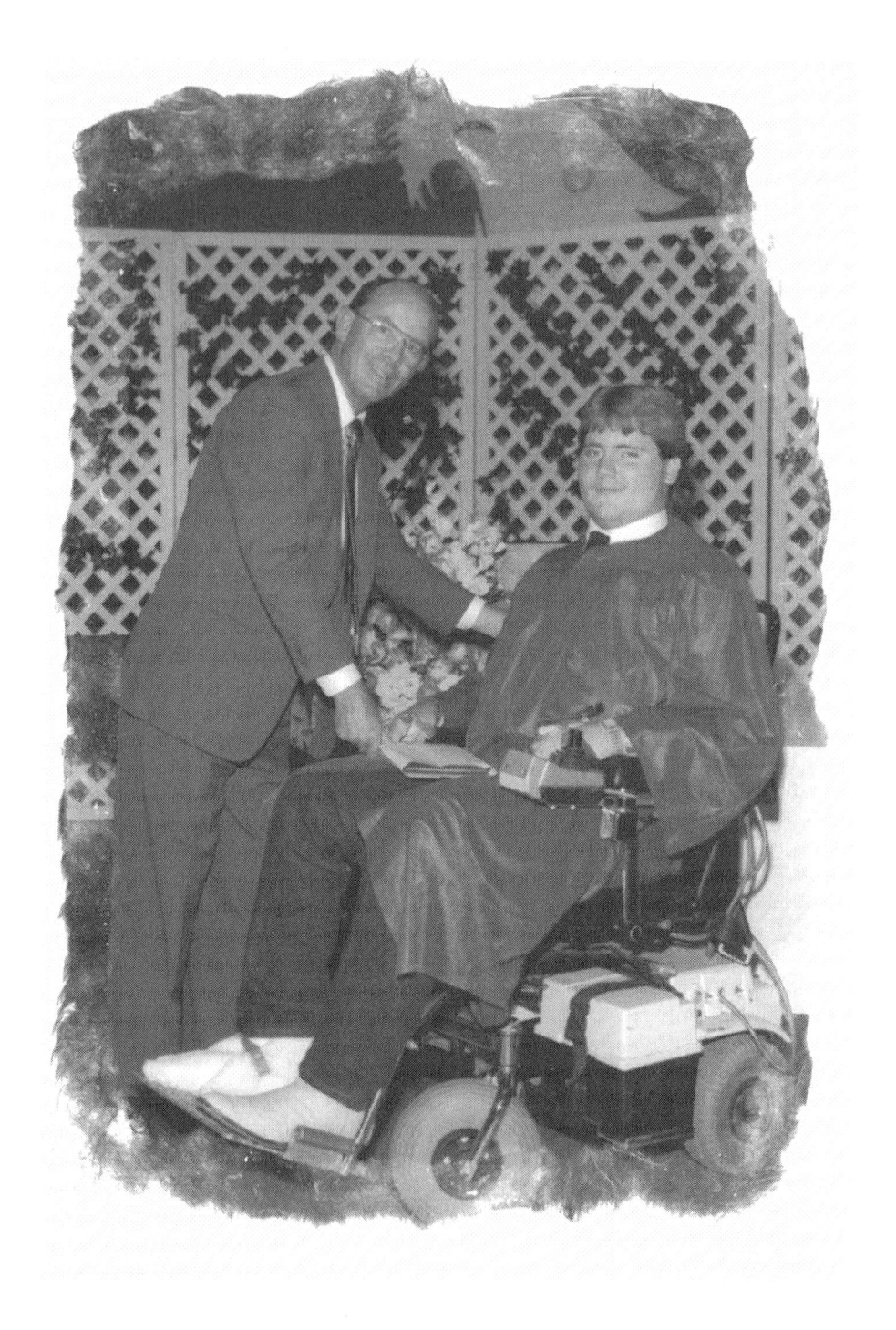

THAT DIPLOMA WAS A LOT OF VERY HARD WORK FOR BOTH TODD AND OUR
FRIEND LAVERNE WHO HELPED HIM CATCH UP ON ALL THE WORK HE MISSED

THIS PICTURE SAYS IT ALL FOR ME – GRADUATION AND LOOKING
TOWARD A NEW AND BRIGHT FUTURE

THE SENIOR GRADUATING CLASS OF 1988

MY SISTER SHARON, TODD, ME — WE HAD A LOT OF FUN

TONI QUIZAR'S 17TH BIRTHDAY

SKIING TRIP WITH MY FRIEND SHIRLEY
TODD, STACY AND EVERYONE ELSE THAT WERE WITH US HAD A GREAT TIME!

YEAH... I'M NOT AWAKE YET AND YET YOU'RE TAKING MY PICTURE?

(LEFT) TODD WAS INVITED TO PARTICIPATE IN A PARADE
(RIGHT) AT A FRIEND'S PARTY

TODD IN HIS BEDROOM WAITING PATIENTLY WITH BILLY BOB

EVEN THOUGH TODD'S DREAMS HAD TO CHANGE, HE GREW UP TO BE A
MAN THAT ANY MOTHER COULD HAVE BEEN PROUD OF — AND I AM

ONE OF MY LAST MEMORIES OF TODD BEING OUT AND HEALTHY

DARLENE, MY BOSS AT MERLE NORMAN COSMETICS. HOW CAN YOU SAY THANK YOU TO A WOMAN WHO OPENED HER HEART AND UNDERSTOOD MY SITUATION AND HELPED ME THROUGH IT INSTEAD OF ADDING TO MY STRESS, DARLENE MADE THOSE LAST DAYS WITH TODD MORE BEARABLE.

DARLENE

TODD AND TAMI KENISTON

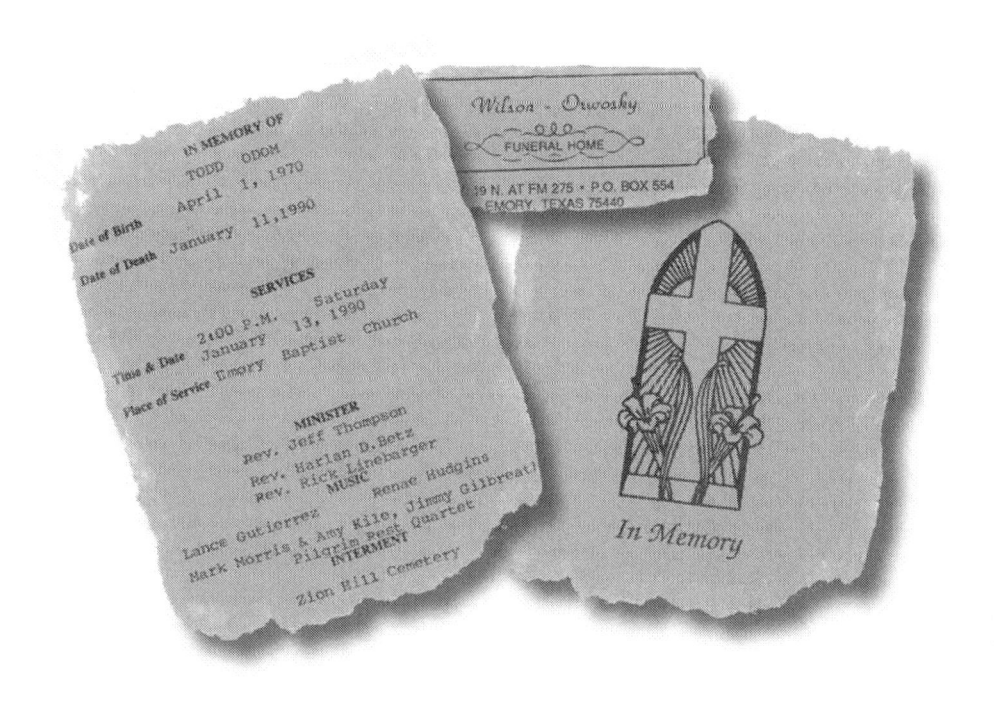

SIX YEARS AFTER TODD'S PASSING. STACY AND I ARE AT A BUSINESS BANQUET.
WE STILL REMEMBER, BUT WE ARE STRONG AND LIVING OUR LIVES.

TODD EDWARD ODOM

AFTERWARD
BUT, WHAT ABOUT ME?

And — that was *Todd... My Son*.

But what about me? Where was I going and what would I do? I would no longer have the labor of love (caring for Todd) consuming my life. I felt as if my own life had ceased to happen as it had all been wrapped up in the caring for my son, and then writing the book, *Todd... My Son*. My every waking moment was caring for Todd. Then it was reliving the memories and writing about him. Now what?

When I walked out of the hospital that day with my daughter, pastor and friends, it was with such a renewed faith in God. In all my life I had not believed as much as I believed in that moment and at that time. Stacy, Laverne, Brother Jeff, Amy and I all walked toward the elevator in complete silence. Todd had gone home and now what?

When we got off the elevator and into the sun that was shining through the Atrium there in the Lobby, we were not sad — we were rejoicing in the name of the Lord as His presence surrounded us. We then began to sing an old hymn from my past, *"On that resurrection morning, when the dead in Christ will rise, I'll have a new body, praise the Lord, I'll have a new life!"* And we walked arm in arm — all of us — out the front door knowing that as surely as I knew there was a heaven, I knew that Todd was no longer bound by that wheelchair! He was standing straight up and walking right into the gates of heaven. And I knew he had been set free from that paralyzed body, now he could soar with the angels.

The atmosphere of the funeral was the same as it was when we walked out of the hospital. The miracle of death had become as great as the miracle of life. *We will live again* if we believe in the Lord Jesus Christ as our Lord and Savior. And we too will roam those streets of gold just as Mark's poem indicated.

There are so many great testimonies that have come out of this story. Way too many to mention here at this time and in this book. There will be another story that will carry us on into the next generation. But for today, I can tell you it has been almost 20 years since Todd went home — and he is as alive in my heart today as the day he left us.

Life has gone on for me...

After Todd's funeral, I continued my career with Merle Norman Cosmetics until the completion of this book. I had written about his death at the hospital and walking out the doors, and the freedom that Stacy and I felt because we knew then that Todd was free.

But I felt that there was supposed to be more to the book. I wanted to express what had happened to me. I knew that there had to be one last chapter in the book that summed up my feelings, that would answer the question burning in my mind, *But, What About Me?*

So, my commitment to writing that last chapter found me in Destin, Florida, at a small hotel on the beach.

I checked in on a Friday and knew that I must complete the last chapter of Todd's book. I knew I had to get this labor of love out of me if I was to go on. And, I knew it would be a long weekend. I asked the clerk not to disturb me as I had work to do. And I labored that whole weekend with the struggles of those last days in my son's life. It was not easy. There were times of crying so hard I didn't think I could breathe or even go on. And then there were moments of laughter with the memories of the past.

Monday morning came and I knew it was time to go back on the road to work but I could not leave — I would not leave — until I had finished that final and most challenging chapter of *Todd... My Son.*

Finally, I called my stepmom, Edith, in Texas and asked her to pray with me so that I could complete this last chapter and move on. We prayed — but still it did not come. I could not write what was pent up inside me.

Feeling a little hopeless and resigned, I thought, *Well, I have not left this room since Friday night, and I'm on the beach — I'll just take a walk.*

So, I walked down to the beach. The morning sun had just begun to peep over the beautiful emerald green waters of the Gulf as I began to pray and cried out to the Lord to help me finish this book. I wanted it done *now*. I did not want to pick it up again at some point in the future and have to finish it then. I wanted to get my story out and close this chapter to my life.

But in that moment I heard in my Spirit, *"It is finished!"*

I said out loud, *"No, Lord, it is NOT finished!"* I hadn't written about what I was feeling, what was going on in my life. So, how could a book that was titled, *Todd... MY Son,* be finished if I wasn't finished telling how I felt about me?

But, I heard again in my Spirit, *"IT IS FINISHED, Todd... My Son is finished!"*

I flung my arms out and screamed out at the water, *"BUT WHAT ABOUT ME?"*

Then I felt the Lord gently speaking into my Spirit.

"But, What About Me? is your next book."

Standing alone on the beach, with the waves coming in, and the breeze blowing cool against my hot face, I felt such a peace settle over me. I knew then that I could go back upstairs, wrap up my belongings and begin the new journey the Lord had in store for me.

It's been a wonderful journey. Yes, there has been sadness, but there's been a lot of joy. I haven't stopped thinking of Todd, and there are times when I miss him dreadfully. But I know that God has my son in his hands and that I will see him one day. It's a great comfort.

And that final chapter that *I thought* was supposed to go into *this book you are holding* — well that has actually turned into another book. It sat on a shelf for a number of years, got dusted off a few times, and now it's about ready. My story has gone on. Stacy married and has two darling little boys. And — I met Jesse Moralez — another story for another time.

God bless you,

Terry Odom-Moralez
August 2009

Well, now you've read my story and you know what a part of my life has been about. And, also that beneath every person's appearance, whether they appear to be well put together or just thrown together, there beats the heart of a person who has to make a choice. You can either lay down and let life beat you up, or you can stand and fight, and press on to do what God has intended for you to do. I hope that through this small book that I have inspired someone to be able to "press on". Because no matter what has happened to you, you can go forward with your life. You don't have to sit down and give up. You can succeed. You will succeed if you just make your mind up and give everything you have, your heart, your sorrows, your everything over to God.

Jesus says, *"Come to Me, all who are weary and heavy-laden, and I will give you rest. Take My yoke upon you and learn from Me, for I am gentle and humble in heart, and you will find rest for your souls. For My yoke is easy and My burden is light."* Mathew 25:28–30 [New American Standard]

Thank you for allowing me to share my story with you. God bless you and *know that God cares for you,* and *He knows you by name.*

Terry Odom-Moralez

TERRY ODOM-MORALEZ WAS A WIFE, MOTHER, AND BUSINESS WOMAN WHEN HER SON, TODD, WAS INJURED IN A DIVING ACCIDENT. SINCE THAT TIME, TERRY HAS GRADUATED FROM VICTORY BIBLE INSTITUTE AND NOW SHARES A MESSAGE OF HOPE THROUGH WRITING AND SPEAKING. TERRY'S GOAL IS TO MOTIVATE WOMEN AND OTHERS TO SEEK GOD WHEN LIFE "HAPPENS" TO THEM. THROUGH HER STORY, SHE HOPES TO REACH HURTING PEOPLE EVERYWHERE AND LET THEM KNOW THEY ARE NOT ALONE IN THEIR STRUGGLES. TO KNOW THAT THERE IS A GOD THEY CAN CALL ON TO HELP, WHO WILL MEET THEM RIGHT WHERE THEY ARE.

YOU CAN FOLLOW TERRY ON FACEBOOK®, TWITTER®, AND OTHER DIGITAL MEDIA.

"DON'T GIVE UP ON
THE BRINK OF A MIRACLE
GOD IS WATCHING YOU
DON'T GIVE UP ON
THE BRINK OF A MIRACLE
HE'LL SEE YOU
THROUGH."

Made in the USA
Charleston, SC
22 September 2010